BACK ROADS
OF OREGON

W9-AHG-809

Log barn at Cornucopia

Back Roads of Oregon
by Earl Thollander

82 Trips on Oregon's Scenic Byways

UPDATED EDITION

SASQUATCH BOOKS
Seattle

Books by Earl Thollander
BACK ROADS OF OREGON
BACK ROADS OF WASHINGTON
BACK ROADS OF CALIFORNIA
BACK ROADS OF THE CAROLINAS
BACK ROADS OF TEXAS
ARIZONA'S SCENIC BYWAYS
BACK ROADS OF NEW ENGLAND
EARL THOLLANDER'S BACK ROADS OF CALIFORNIA
EARL THOLLANDER'S SAN FRANCISCO

Note: Anyone noticing discrepancies in the maps or changes in roads is invited to write to the author at 19210 Highway 128, Calistoga, Ca., 94515.

Copyright ©1993 by Earl Thollander.
Updated Edition.

All rights reserved. No part of this book may be reproduced or utilized in any form or by any means without the written permission of the publisher.

Originally published in 1979 by Clarkson N. Potter, Inc.

Cover illustration: The forest road near Steamboat, on the way to Applegate. By Earl Thollander

Library of Congress Cataloging in Publication Data
Thollander, Earl.
    Back roads of Oregon : 82 trips on Oregon's scenic byways / by Earl Thollander.—Updated ed.
        p.   cm.
    Originally published: New York : Clarkson N. Potter, 1979.
    ISBN 0-912365-77-3 : $12.95
    1. Oregon—Guidebooks. 2. Automobile travel—Oregon—Guidebooks.
I. Title.
F874.3.T48   1993
917.9504'43—dc20   92-42589
                                              CIP

Published by Sasquatch Books
1931 Second Avenue
Seattle, Washington 98101
(206) 441-5555

Printed in Hong Kong

I dedicate this book,
with much love, to my
family—Janet, Kristie,
Wes and Lauren

Contents

Back Roads of Northwestern Oregon

Back Roads of Eastern Oregon

Map legend

.   3.2   .   distance in miles between dots

→ → →   my route (which may be reversed should you desire.)

▲ campgrounds
■ towns and cities
·············· rivers and lake boundaries
□ special location
✗ my sketching place
⌂ covered bridge
⊼ picnic grounds
⊞ cemetery

NORTH is always toward the top of the page

Preface

Back Roads of Oregon is a travel guide, an on-the-spot pictorial record of landscapes and places seen, and an effort to give "voice" to the back road beauty of Oregon. For me there is more of nature, more experience of the earth, a greater feeling of history, and more good adventures to be had by getting off the main thoroughfares and away from urban centers.

I drew this book not only because of an urge to describe to everyone what wonderful things I have seen in Oregon, but also to help others, in my small way, discover the beauty of the natural world. Without strong support from concerned people, preserving and managing the natural areas that remain will be difficult. Indeed without care and help we will someday create a less interesting and less habitable planet.

Oregon was a truly varied, beautiful, and inspiring state to visit via the back roads.

I'm concerned about the preservation of our earth and have concluded that progress can only be defined in terms of how close we can come to living in harmony with nature. At a time when mankind has so many earth-destroying processes going on we often seem to be moving backward rather than ahead, Oregon has remained relatively unspoiled.

I believe that in order to advance and develop as a proud nation we need to restore the elemental beauty and purpose of nature, make healthy and pure our air and water, and preserve Oregon's and our heritage and history wherever and whenever possible. The needs of the planet earth should now supersede those of mankind.

Earl Thollander

Thanks to artist John Simpkins and son Wes Thollander who were welcome company on my 6,000 mile back road journey through Oregon.

Author's Note

The three parts of *Back Roads of Oregon* begin with a sectional map. This will help to locate the back roads areas on a larger Oregon state map that is available at no charge from many sources, including Travel Services, Chambers of Commerce, Tourist Bureaus and Automobile Clubs. My more localized maps in each section outline every back road and should successfully guide you in your trip.

I have put as much information as I could manage into the maps themselves. Arrows show you the direction in which I traveled, although my route could certainly be reversed. The North Pole, unless otherwise indicated, is toward the top of the page. Maps are not to scale because of the diversity in length of the roads; however, mileage notations should help a great deal. My odometer wouldn't have measured distance exactly the same as yours, but their estimates should be similar. Essential to me in following the back roads were sectional maps, which I purchased from the Oregon Department of Transportation, Room 17, Transportation Building, Salem, Oregon 97310. Pasted together, the various sections of a county map, at one half inch to the mile, would achieve monumental proportions. Malheur County alone, for example, measured 30 x 75 inches!

I also purchased maps at ranger stations when entering forest preserves. They are a bit more complete than the Department's sectional maps in that forest road numbers are included.

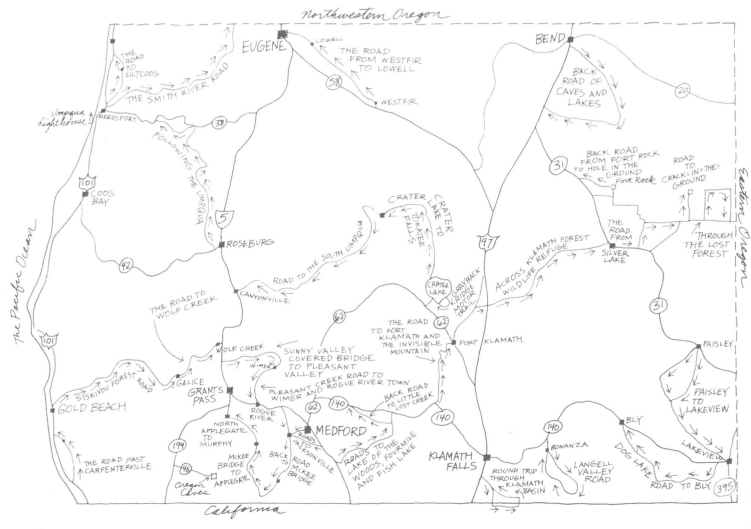

Rhododendron —

Southwestern
Oregon

I remember the beauty and
force of the ocean coast, the
forests gleaming with dew
in the morning light,
the sumptuous displays of
mountain wildflowers, and the
textural infinity of sagebrush mixed with
pines and junipers in the high, dry
portion of southwestern Oregon.

13

View from the Ridge

The road past Carpenterville

Old Highway 101, called the Carpenterville Road, wound above the ocean shore through lush, green coastal forest. It became a ridge road at times with dramatic views to both east and west. Be careful of cows on the road, and cats. I came across a cluster of eight half-grown black cats. Once they scattered, I could proceed. Carpenterville itself seems to have vanished.

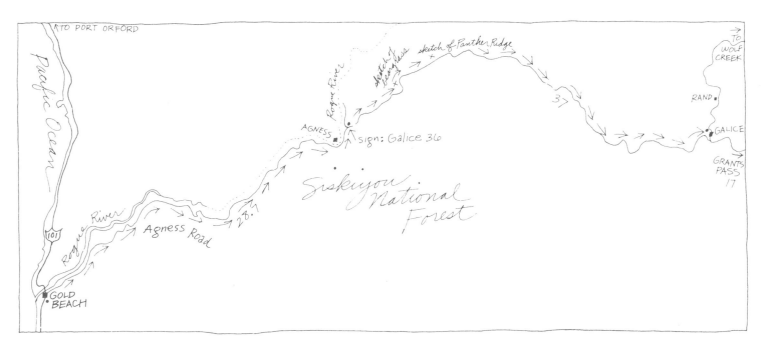

TO PORT ORFORD

Pacific Ocean

Rogue River

Agness Road

Rogue River

AGNESS

sign: Galice 36

28.1

Siskiyou National Forest

101

GOLD BEACH

sketch of Panther Ridge

sketch of leany pass

37

TO WOLF CREEK

RAND

GALICE

GRANTS PASS 17

Stonecrop

Siskiyou Forest Road, Gold Beach to Galice

I stopped at Gold Beach Ranger Station for a Siskiyou National Forest map.

From the road beside the Rogue River, I watched a power boat moving upstream at almost the same speed as I was traveling.

Past Agness the road wound its way through deep forest.

Eventually I came across an area of many beargrass plants. Not until I sketched the white blossoms did I discover an equally white spider with its victim, an unsuspecting yellow and black wasp.

I had expansive views of mountains and forest for my drawing of distant Panther Ridge.

Beargrass

Panther Ridge

WILLIAM
MILLER
—
TENNESSEE
—
20 D
20,

Headstone at Wolf Creek
cemetery

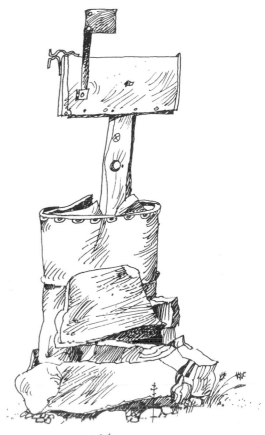

mailbox on
Wolf Creek
road

The road to Wolf Creek

I took the road north from Galice
along the Rogue, turning east at Grave Creek
Bridge. In five miles I passed a nicely made
log barn and also a sign that said "No shooting
children and livestock." Turning at the fork of
the road toward Wolf Creek, I traveled along
the pretty stream to the sleepy town ahead
where old Wolf Creek Tavern (1857) still stands.
On a hill nearby I sat in the deep shade
of the town cemetery to sketch an
ivy-covered headstone.

Sunny Valley covered bridge to Pleasant Valley

Sunny Valley covered bridge crosses Grave Creek, so named in memory of a fourteen-year-old pioneer, buried nearby, a member of the first wagon train to enter Oregon by the Applegate Trail in 1846.

A small boy I met who lived on a farm along the road told me that there were beavers in the creek.

I got advice along the way from local folks and abandoned the Daisy Mine Road upon hearing their cautionary "This yere road's so rough ye could berry yer wheel in one 'o them holes."

Meadows along Ditch Creek Road were sprinkled with countless daisies blooming in late spring.

Sunny Valley
covered bridge

23

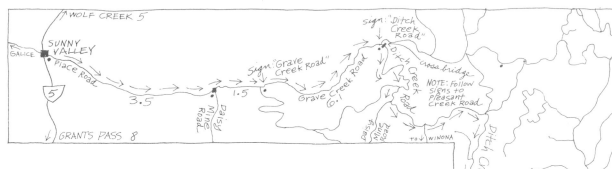

Pleasant Creek Road to Wimer
and Rogue River town

At 2383 Pleasant Creek Road
I sketched a portion of a
collection of old structures
and felt fully immersed
in the spirit of Oregon's
past. Grapevines and
roses flourished, and
peacocks, ducks, cats,
and a friendly dog
roamed about the
thick grass.

farm on
Pleasant Creek
Road

25

Roads to Jacksonville

Jacksonville is a small, historic town revived by a remarkable number of handsomely restored houses and other edifaces that are well worth seeing.

I sketched the 1884 former Jackson County Courthouse, the seat of county government until 1927. It was proclaimed, originally, the "crowning glory of Jacksonville."

The Jacksonville Courthouse, 1884

28 St. Joseph's Church, Jacksonville

Roads to Jacksonville

St. Joseph's Church (1858) at 4th and D streets in Jacksonville was on the list of things to see. It's a historical place, as you can tell from this excerpt from a report by the town's first Catholic missionary to his superior, Archbishop Francis Blanchet ...

Sept. 18, 1856

... the Catholics in Jacksonville are very anxious to have a church built amongst them and are willing to help to the utmost of their means. I have given them some hopes of having their wishes realized next year ... Next spring, if the mining be successful this winter, there would be a fair chance of making a good collection toward building a little church, which will answer not only for that town but for all the mining districts for 60 or 70 miles all around.

Back road from Jacksonville to Buncom and McKee Bridge

This was a pleasant trip past stream and forest. At ghostly Buncom cows grazed in the green meadow where the town once stood. Next, I traveled along the Little Applegate River, and then by the big Applegate to McKee Bridge.

The covered bridge was built in 1917 when the Blue Ledge Copper Mine was still transporting ore to Jacksonville.

I could hear the swishing sound of a rotary fish screen operating much like an old-fashioned water wheel as I sketched. The screen prevents trout from going out of the river into irrigation canals and ending up "dried out" in a pasture somewhere.

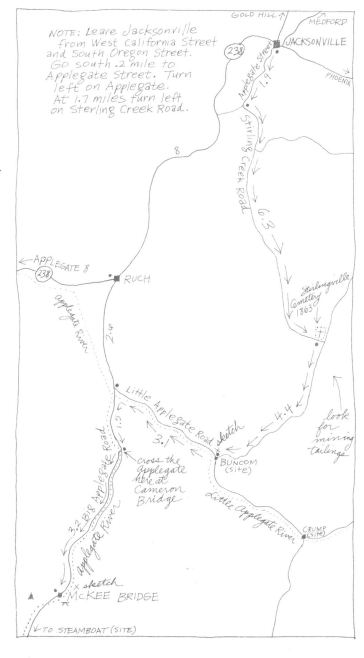

NOTE: Leave Jacksonville from West California Street and South Oregon Street. Go south .2 mile to Applegate Street. Turn left on Applegate. At 1.7 miles turn left on Sterling Creek Road.

GOLD HILL

MEDFORD

JACKSONVILLE

238

Applegate Street

1.9

PHOENIX

Stirling Creek Road

8

6.3

← APPLEGATE 8
238

RUCH

Applegate River

2.0

Stirlingville Cemetery 1863

4.4

look for mining tailings

Little Applegate Road

sketch

1.5

3.1

cross the Applegate here at Cameron Bridge

BUNCOM (site)

Little Applegate River

CRUMP (site)

3.2 B18 Applegate Road

Applegate River

X sketch

McKEE BRIDGE

↓ TO STEAMBOAT (SITE)

Buncom

McKee Bridge to Applegate via Steamboat

Once past the Applegate Lake
reservoir the road was
picturesque, with meadows,
streams and, near the site
of Steamboat, with
overhanging forest trees.
Along Thompson Creek
toward Applegate there
were many great barns
and farms in lovely
pastoral settings.

McKee covered bridge

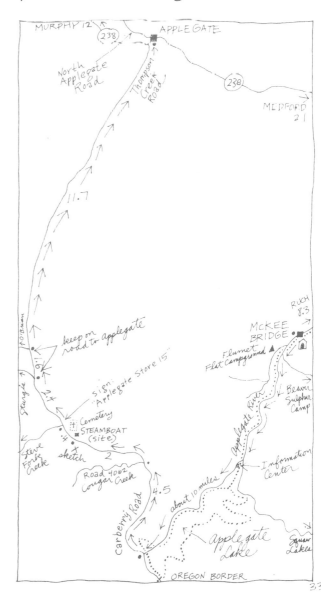

34   The road near Steamboat

35

The Krause barn, North Applegate Road

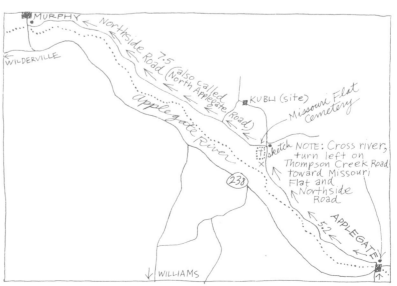

MURPHY

WILDERVILLE

Northside Road

7.5 (also called (North Applegate) Road)

KUBLI (site)

Missouri Flat Cemetery

Applegate River

sketch NOTE: Cross river, turn left on Thompson Creek Road toward Missouri Flat and Northside Road

238

APPLEGATE

5.2

↓ WILLIAMS

North Applegate Road to Murphy

This byway is also called Northside Road.
It goes past meadows and barns and then idles by
the Missouri Flat cemetery where "Artesian Water
A Gift from God" was offered. In 1943 Bert Clute
donated the water system in memory of his wife, Lydia.
The good water was a gift, indeed.

Roads to Lake of the Woods, Fourmile and Fish Lake

Dead Indian Road, off Highway 66 a mile or so south of Ashland, is scenic all the way to Lake of the Woods. Highway 140 off Highway 62 six miles north of Medford goes to Fish Lake, Lake of the Woods and past the dirt road turnoff to Fourmile Lake.

There are views of Mt. McLoughlin and I sketched the classic peak with an early morning mist mantling its base.

McLoughlin is not a popular name with old-timers in this area because he favored the British, so they say. Their name for the 9500-foot mountain was Snowy Butte, and later, Mt. Pitt.

Mount McLoughlin

Back road to Little Lost Creek

There is a quiet back road paralleling Highway 140 through the Rogue River National Forest. It begins opposite the Big Elk Guard Station near Fish Lake. Ask about the condition of the road at the Guard Station as conditions may vary from season to season and year to year. The road eventually winds (a bit precariously) down into a green valley along the south fork of Little Butte Creek. Southeast of the tiny community of Lakecreek the road past Little Lost Creek branches off one mile to Oregon's "shortest covered bridge."

There was no traffic over the old span as I sketched. A rooster crowed, a fly bit me, green dragonflies whirred by, and spiders lowered themselves onto my drawing paper from an overhanging alder tree.

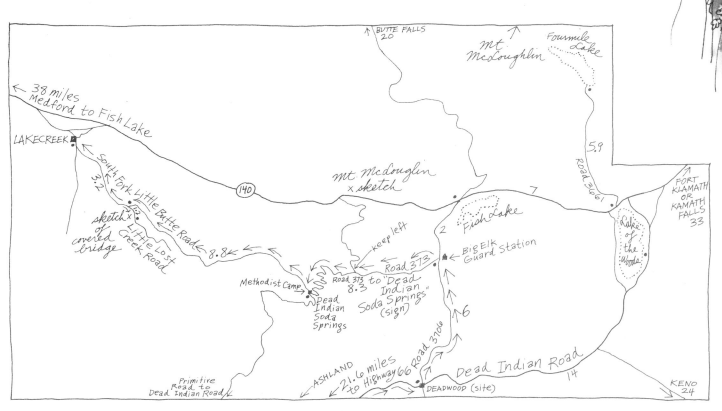

Little Lost Creek
Covered Bridge

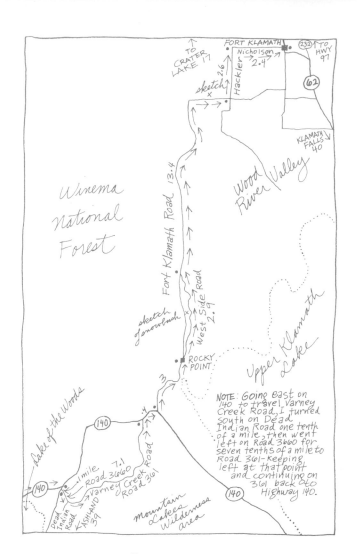

Winema
National
Forest

Fort Klamath Road 13.4

sketch of snowbank ×

West Side Road 2.9

Lake of the Woods

ROCKY POINT

Upper Klamath Lake

Wood River Valley

FORT KLAMATH

Nicholson 2.4

Hackler 2.6

TO CRATER LAKE 17

sketch ×

(232) TO HWY 97

(62)

KLAMATH FALLS 40

NOTE: Going east on 140 to travel Varney Creek Road, I turned south on Dead Indian Road one tenth of a mile, then went left on Road 3660 for seven tenths of a mile to Road 3661—keeping left at that point and continuing on 3661 back to Highway 140.

(140)

(140)

(140)

Dead Indian Road

ASHLAND 39

1 mile

Road 3660

Varney Creek Road 3661

Mountain Lakes Wilderness area

(140)

View from Klamath Meadows

The road to Fort Klamath and the Invisible Mountain

From Lake of the Woods, Varney Creek Road
parallels Highway 140, a quiet forest drive. At
Rocky Point I turned off the Fort Klamath
Road for the slower pace of West Side Road.
In June the sweetly fragrant snowbush lined the
roadside. Later, crossing Fort Klamath Meadows,
I sketched the broad view looking north toward the
region of Crater Lake and the now invisible
Mt. Mazama, which once dominated this
landscape. Indian legend tells of a great
eruption and the collapse of the former
15,000-foot Mt. Mazama, a story
supported by geologists.

Snowbush

Crater Lake and Grayback Ridge Motor Nature Trail

Indian legend best describes Crater Lake to me. The medicine men of Klamath, who were the only people the Spirit Chief allowed to visit the lake, pictured it as a giant cave..."The cave is deep and bottomless, as deep and bottomless as the sky. The mountains around it sink far into the earth and reach toward the clouds. The cave is filled with blue water--water of a deeper blue than the sky which looks at itself in the lake."*

Grayback Ridge Motor Trail is through a mountain hemlock, lodgepole pine, and mixed conifer forest. On my trip chipmunks bounded across the road and fat black and gray birds, pine nut loving "Clark's Nutcrackers," were much in evidence. There were long views of Matterhorn like Union Peak, Mt. McLoughlin, Crater Peak and faraway Mt. Shasta.

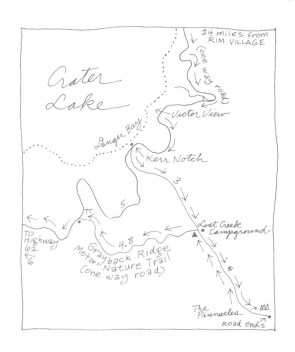

Crater Lake

24 miles from RIM VILLAGE

(one way road)

Victor View

Danger Bay

Kerr Notch

3

5

TT

TO Highway 62

4.8

Grayback Ridge Motor Nature Trail (one way road)

Lost Creek Campground

The Pinnacles Road ends

*from Indian Legends of the Pacific Northwest, by Ella E. Clark; Copyright 1953, The Regents of the University of California; reprinted by permission of the University of California Press.

Crater Lake

45

High bluffs near
Toketee Falls

46

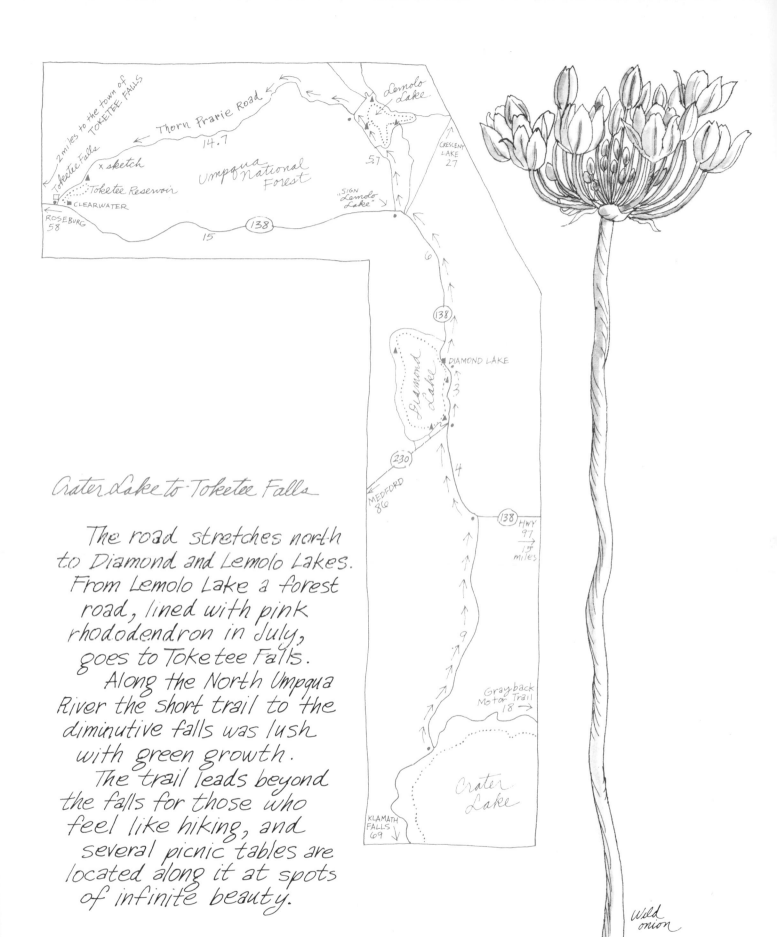

Crater Lake to Toketee Falls

The road stretches north to Diamond and Lemolo Lakes. From Lemolo Lake a forest road, lined with pink rhododendron in July, goes to Toketee Falls.

Along the North Umpqua River the short trail to the diminutive falls was lush with green growth.

The trail leads beyond the falls for those who feel like hiking, and several picnic tables are located along it at spots of infinite beauty.

Wild onion

Tiger Lily

Blackberry

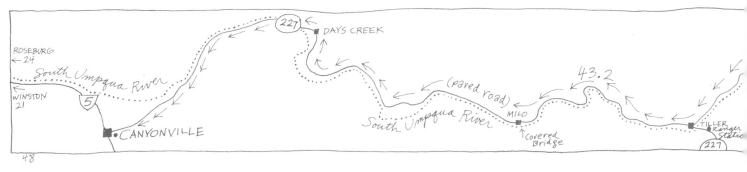

ROSEBURG
← 24

WINSTON
21

5

South Umpqua River

CANYONVILLE

227

DAYS CREEK

(paved road)

South Umpqua River

MILO

Covered
Bridge

43.2

TILLER
Ranger
Station

227

Road to the South Umpqua River

This is a forest drive lined with yarrow, lupine, and elderberry along the roadside. I stopped to draw a brilliant orange tiger lily. At South Umpqua Falls I had a swim before sitting down to draw. Young people were diving and tumbling over the falls, and a group of boys in five truck inner tubes held onto each other as they went over the falls. I had some doubts about their safety, but in the tangle of tubes, bodies, and churning water, they survived with much shouting and laughter.

ROSEBURG 50

CLEARWATER 7.8

138

SIGN: "BIG CAMAS"

Road 2734
Copeland Creek Road

× flower sketches

(unpaved road)

13.5

Road 2734

Rhododendron Ridge

Umpqua National Forest

FRENCH JUNCTION 4800'

Buckhead Mountain

Canyon Road 2734

Rolling Grounds Camp

13.5

Black Rock Fork

Deer Lick Falls

Castle Rock Fork

Road 2734

Road 2838

4.4

South Umpqua River

Road 284

South Umpqua Falls sketch

Campbell Falls

South Umpqua River

Umpqua National Forest

Starflower

49

South Umpqua Falls

51

Brambles in
the window

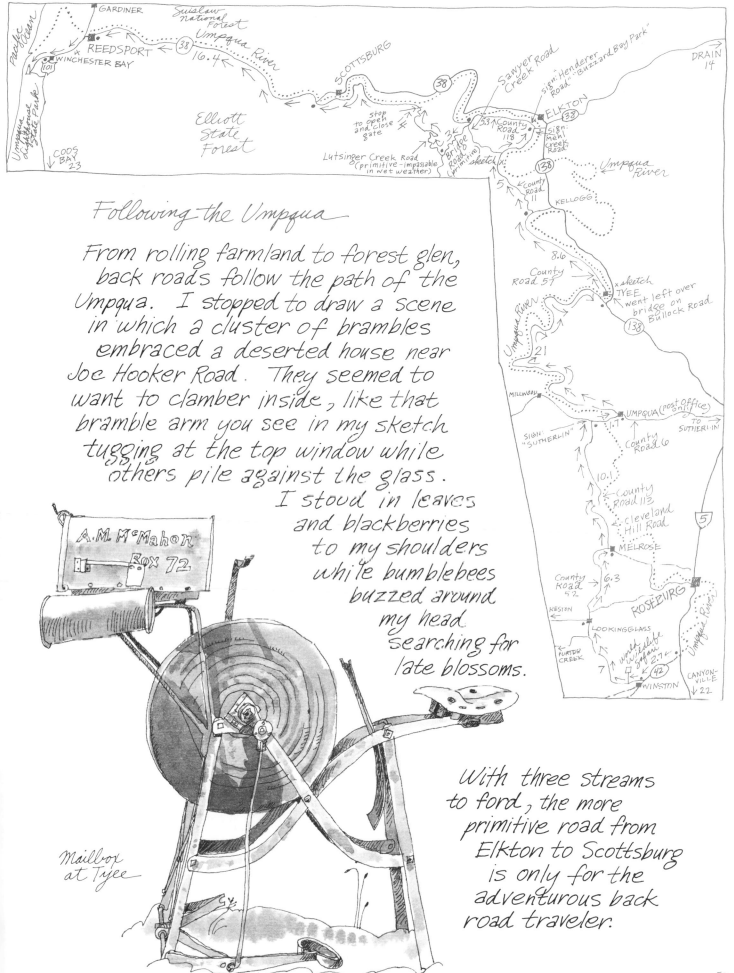

Following the Umpqua

From rolling farmland to forest glen, back roads follow the path of the Umpqua. I stopped to draw a scene in which a cluster of brambles embraced a deserted house near Joe Hooker Road. They seemed to want to clamber inside, like that bramble arm you see in my sketch tugging at the top window while others pile against the glass.

I stood in leaves and blackberries to my shoulders while bumblebees buzzed around my head searching for late blossoms.

Mailbox at Tyee

With three streams to ford, the more primitive road from Elkton to Scottsburg is only for the adventurous back road traveler.

A.M. McMahon Box 72

COAST GUARD

The little road to Umpqua River Lighthouse

Near Reedsport the Umpqua finally empties into the Pacific Ocean. The nicely proportioned Umpqua River Lighthouse was built in 1939. Its 1,800,000-candlepower light can be seen for twenty miles.

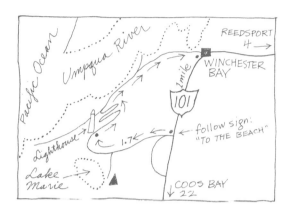

Umpqua River Lighthouse

The road to Siltcoos

Here are views of lakes and inlets filled with pond lilies, rushes, old stumps, and ancient mossy logs.

Indians called the yellow-blossomed pond lily I sketched "Wocus," and roasted and ate the large seeds--if ducks didn't get to them first! Trout prefer the cool water under the pond lilies. To fishermen, the wocus indicates that the water is likely to be too deep for wading in hip boots.

"Wocus,"
Indian pond lily

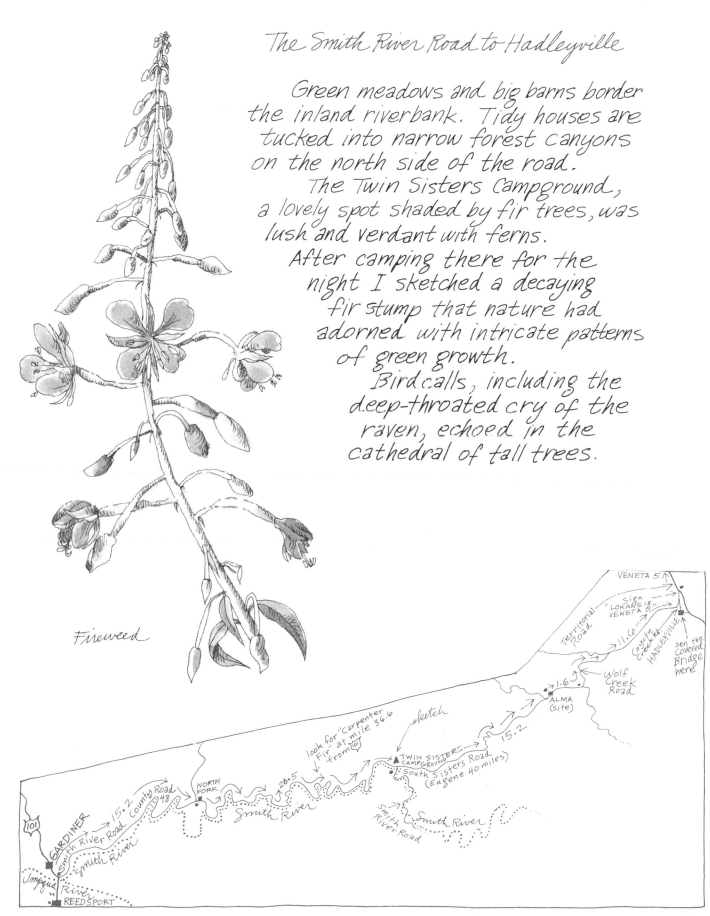

The Smith River Road to Hadleyville

Green meadows and big barns border the inland riverbank. Tidy houses are tucked into narrow forest canyons on the north side of the road.

The Twin Sisters Campground, a lovely spot shaded by fir trees, was lush and verdant with ferns.

After camping there for the night I sketched a decaying fir stump that nature had adorned with intricate patterns of green growth.

Birdcalls, including the deep-throated cry of the raven, echoed in the cathedral of tall trees.

Fireweed

Stump at
Twin Sisters

58

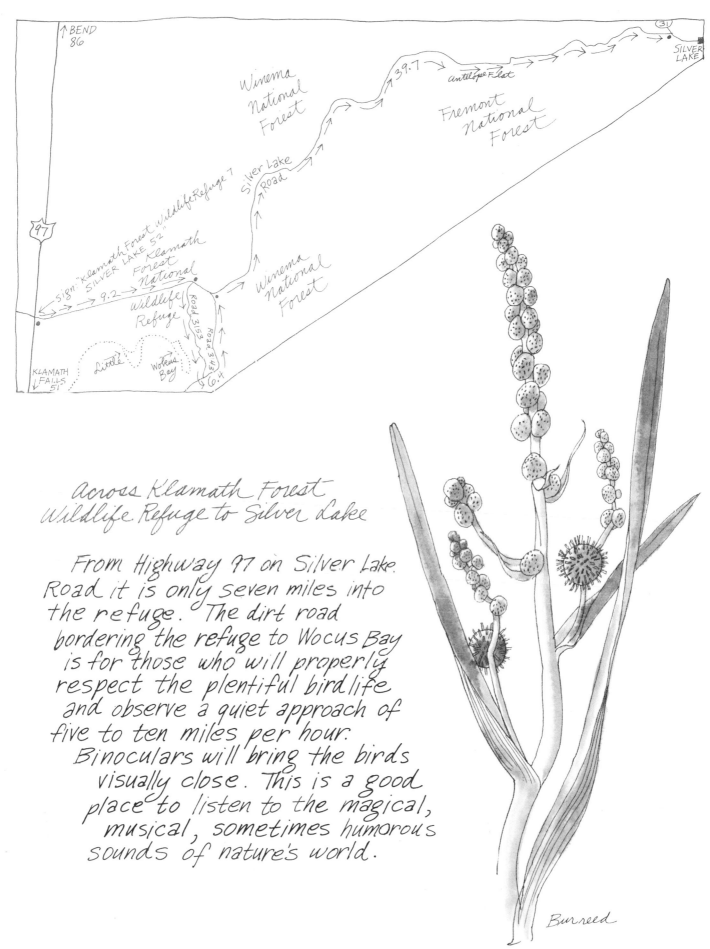

Across Klamath Forest
Wildlife Refuge to Silver Lake

From Highway 97 on Silver Lake
Road it is only seven miles into
the refuge. The dirt road
bordering the refuge to Wocus Bay
is for those who will properly
respect the plentiful bird life
and observe a quiet approach of
five to ten miles per hour.
Binoculars will bring the birds
visually close. This is a good
place to listen to the magical,
musical, sometimes humorous
sounds of nature's world.

Burreed

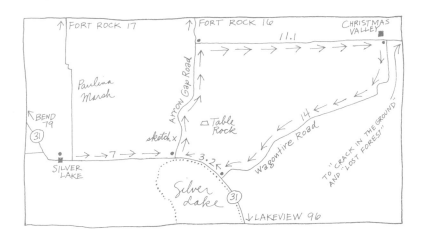

The road from Silver Lake

Arrow Gap Road out of Silver Lake
afforded one of the many views of
distinctive Table Rock. From
any direction it was admirable
in its proportions.

Table Rock

Road to Crack-in-the-Ground

The big crack was not that easy to find, being rather poorly marked. For this reason I have made the mileage count as accurately as possible for you. There's an interesting variation in temperature from warm to icy as you proceed to walk into the crack. In fact, the interior is so cool that early settlers used to come here for ice when everything else had melted away.

While I was sketching I was startled by a sudden fluttering of wings, and a Red-Shafted-Flicker zoomed through the crack, swerving as he narrowly missed my head.

A bit farther on this road you will see lava deposits. Then it is best to return the way you came. I went around the lava flow through miles and miles of sagebrush only generally knowing where I was. With a deteriorating passageway ahead, by luck I was able to find my way back to Christmas Valley.

miles and miles of sagebrush

Crack-in-the-Ground

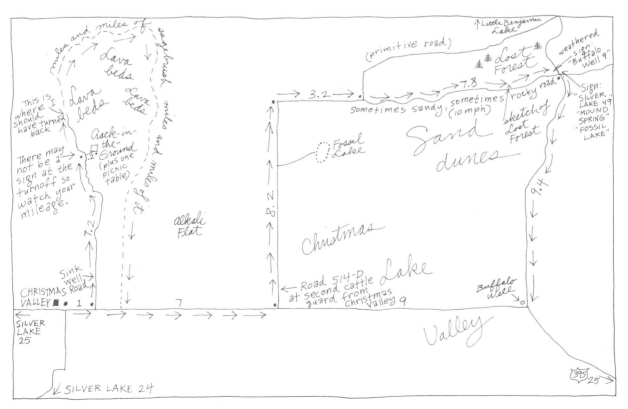

miles and miles of

sagebrush miles and miles of

Lava beds

Lava beds

Lava beds

This is where I should have turned back

There may not be a sign at the turnoff so watch your mileage.

Crack-in-the-Ground (plus one picnic table)

.2

7.2

Sink Well Road

CHRISTMAS VALLEY ■ ● 1 ●

Alkali Flat

7

20 N

Christmas

← Road 514-D at second cattle guard from Christmas Valley 9

Lake

Valley

↑ Little Benjamin Lake

(primitive road)

→ 3.2 →

sometimes sandy, sometimes rocky road (10 mph)

→ 7.8

Fossil Lake

Lost Forest

weathered sign "Buffalo Well 9"

Sign: SILVER LAKE 49 "MOUND SPRING" "FOSSIL LAKE"

sketch of Lost Forest

Sand dunes

9.4

Buffalo Well ○

SILVER LAKE 25

↓ SILVER LAKE 24

395 25 →

The Lost Forest

Through the Lost Forest

This is a primitive road and a bit far from civilization. The trip goes past Fossil Lake, where important fossils were found in the late 1800s.

The Lost Forest is a unique stand of ponderosa pine growing forty miles from other forests in an area so dry that the trees only receive one-half the rainfall that they would normally need. Some of the largest junipers in Oregon also grow here.

Back road from Fort Rock to Hole-in-the-Ground

Fort Rock really is fortresslike, and it is possible to take a somewhat precarious rim drive within the rock's interior. To the west of the rock is a butte enclosing a cave where an archeologist discovered ancient Indian sandals. These were radio-carbon dated at more than 10,000 years, making them the oldest evidence of human habitation in Oregon.

Hole-in-the-Ground, one mile wide, 300 feet deep, was formed by a violent volcanic eruption. The pattern of sagebrush and trees within the hole is striking to contemplate.

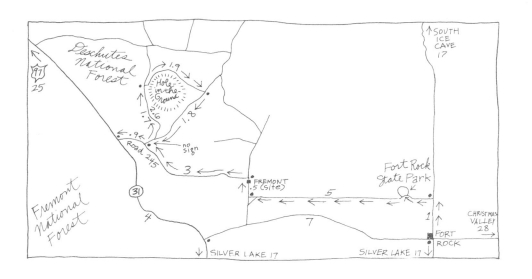

Fort Rock

In Paisley I drew the
United Methodist Church
on Mill Street. It
was completed and
dedicated in 1901, and
is still serving this
small community.
To the right in my
picture, I included
a wagon-wheel
fence cleverly
decorated with
horseshoes.

The church on Mill Street, Paisley.

Old settler's cabin in the meadow

There were two roads from Paisley into Fremont National Forest. On the high road, in an alpine meadow near Puppy Dog Springs, was this old structure surrounded by grass and wildflowers. On a sunny day in June, when the birds are in strong and sweet voice, it is as good a place to be as anywhere on earth.

Sign: "Campbell Lake 22 Deadhorse Lake 23"

SILVER LAKE 50

PAISLEY

Road 331

Road 331

Road 330

8.2

.9

2.0

Bear Creek

31

Road 348

sketched

13.4

Coffeepot Springs

LAKEVIEW 45

Note: Watch for logging trucks!

Sign "LAKEVIEW 39"

Road 337

Road 348

Road 330

22

6.2 Happy Camp

Road 2823

DAIRY POINT

Road 348 BLY 20

2.1

Fremont National Forest

Road 2823

Sign: "LAKEVIEW 31"

45 PAISLEY

31

395

Road 2823

KLAMATH FALLS 96

140

LAKEVIEW

ALTURAS 40

Juniper

Dog Lake Road to Bly

I must have stayed at Dog Lake's Cinder Hill Camp on the wrong night of the week. The mosquitoes were particularly voracious. However, an old fisherman told me the fishing was good. He had a freezer in his trailer and already had a good stock of fish packed away. Along this forest road I sketched a juniper and a big mule-ears blossom. There were thousands of white pond buttercups on the pond surface at Robinson Spring. A black duck paddled through all the whiteness. I dripped a blob of black ink on my drawing while striking at a mosquito.

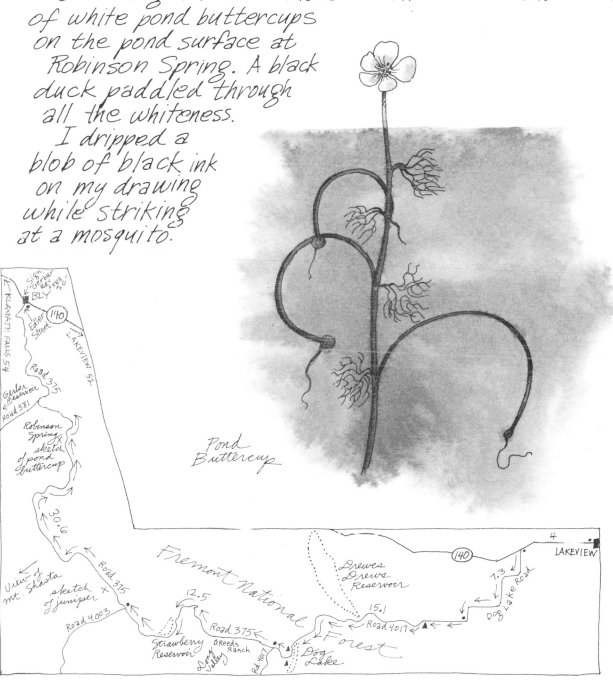

Pond Buttercup

The old Fitzhugh place,
Langell Valley

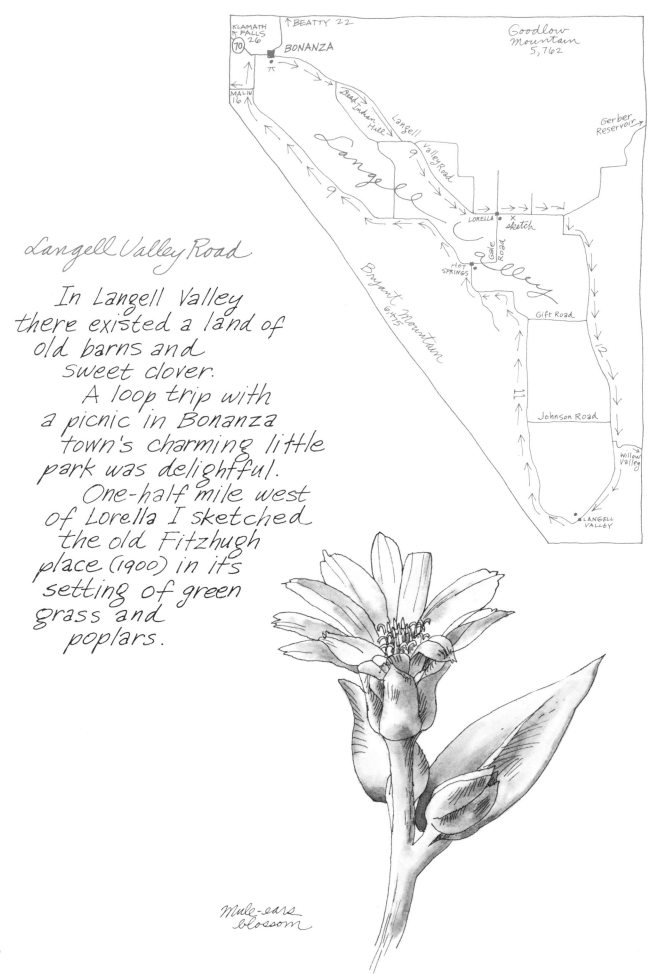

Langell Valley Road

In Langell Valley there existed a land of old barns and sweet clover.

A loop trip with a picnic in Bonanza town's charming little park was delightful.

One-half mile west of Lorella I sketched the old Fitzhugh place (1900) in its setting of green grass and poplars.

Mule-ears blossom

Round trip through Klamath Basin

There is much drama and many interesting sights along the canals and waterways south of Klamath Falls. Egrets were stationed at intervals along Klamath Strait Drain Outlet, each rising to flight as I traveled slowly down the levee road. Groups of cormorants flew between the dikes, geese scurried to the water to swim to the other side, hawks lay in wait to capture ducklings, and a great white pelican took off into the wind, pushing at the water surface for takeoff speed.

Typical comments by visitors in the Refuge Visitor Register were "Beyond fantastic," "Praise the Lord," "Avocet sounds are super.," and my own notation, "Hooray for the birds."

Birds of the Klamath Basin

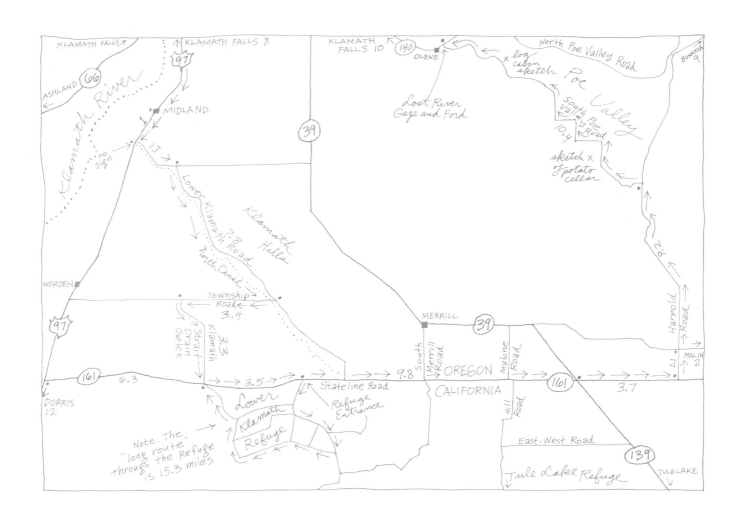

KLAMATH FALLS→ ↑ ←KLAMATH FALLS 8 KLAMATH FALLS 10 140 OLENE North Poe Valley Road BONANZA 9

ASHLAND 66 Klamath River 97 ×log cabin sketch Poe Valley

Lost River Gap and Ford South Poe Valley Road 10.4

MIDLAND 39 sketch × ↑potato cellar

no sign 1.7 Lower Klamath Road 7.8 Klamath Hills

North Canal

WORDEN Township Road 3.4 9.2

97 Strait Drain Outlet 3.3 Klamath MERRILL 39 Malone Road Harpold Road

161 6.3 3.5 9.8 South Merrill Road OREGON 161 3.7 1.1 MALIN 2

DORRIS 12 Stateline Road CALIFORNIA Hill Road

Lower Klamath Refuge Refuge Entrance

Note: The "long route" through the Refuge is 15.3 miles East-West Road 139

Tule Lake Refuge TULELAKE

Potato Cellar

Within Poe Valley, and indeed in all the
farming country hereabouts, are potato cellars.
Farmers can store potatoes in these
insulated half-barns from
September to April.

I drew the trapper's cabin on the site of a Modoc Indian campground. Sam High originally purchased the land from the first homesteader in about 1880. Sam High's grandson told me the cabin is known to have been there in 1860.

In returning to Highway 140 on this round trip through Klamath Basin, a bridge crosses the Lost River fording place used by the earliest travelers in this section of Oregon.

Trappers cabin, circa 1860

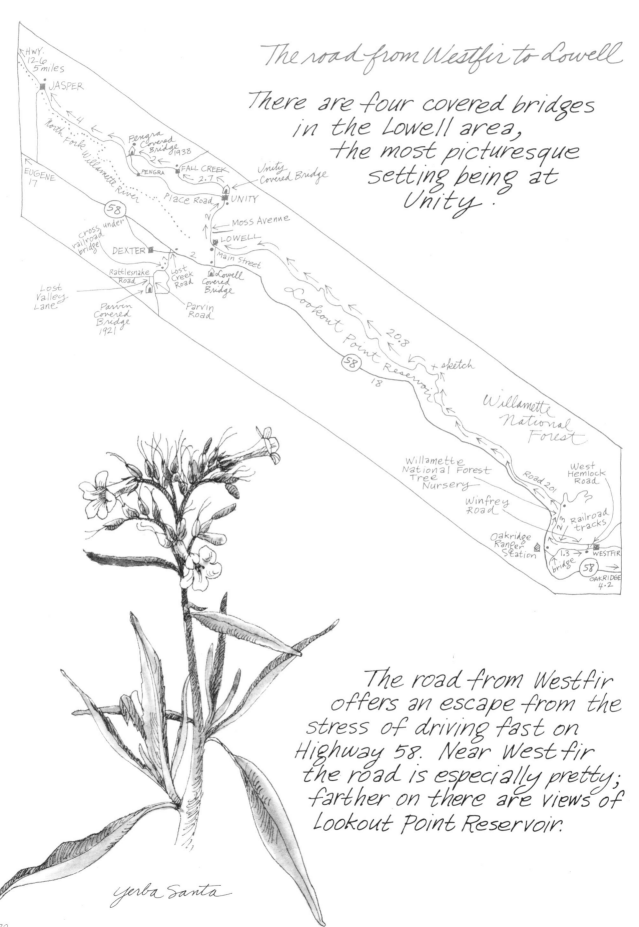

The road from Westfir to Lowell

There are four covered bridges in the Lowell area, the most picturesque setting being at Unity.

HWY. 12-6 5 miles
JASPER
North Fork Willamette River
Pengra Covered Bridge 1938
PENGRA
Fall Creek 2.7
Unity Covered Bridge
EUGENE 17
58
Place Road
UNITY
Moss Avenue
Cross under railroad bridge
DEXTER
LOWELL
Main Street
Rattlesnake Road
Lost Creek Road
Lowell Covered Bridge
Lost Valley Lane
Parvin Covered Bridge 1921
Parvin Road
Lookout Point Reservoir
20.8
58
18
+ sketch
Willamette National Forest
Willamette National Forest Tree Nursery
Road 201
West Hemlock Road
Winfrey Road
Railroad tracks
Oakridge Ranger Station
1.3 bridge
WESTFIR
58
OAKRIDGE 4.2

The road from Westfir offers an escape from the stress of driving fast on Highway 58. Near Westfir the road is especially pretty; farther on there are views of Lookout Point Reservoir.

yerba Santa

The road
from Westfir

Back road of caves and lakes

The landscape was of pine and sagebrush, gently rolling across the high desert.
At Skeleton Cave I sketched by flashlight in the cool interior.
There was much to see in this volcanic area south of Bend.
With stops at four caves, this back road took me to Newberry Crater and its two popular fishing lakes, East and Paulina. Then there was Lava Cast Forest, Lava River Caves, and Lava Butte to visit on the way back to Bend.

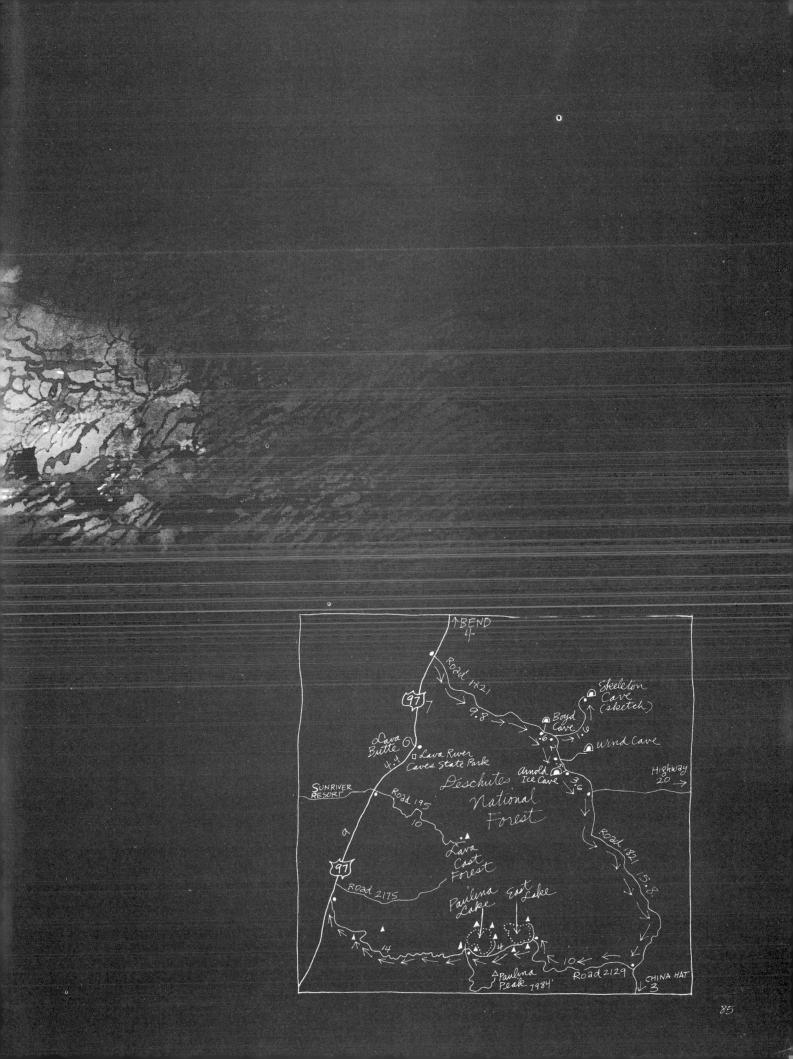

ASTORIA

THE ROAD TO BROWNSMEAD
LEVEE ROAD
SIDE ROAD ON PAST MAYGER

THE ROAD THROUGH FORT STEVENS STATE PARK

YOUNG RIVER AND WALLUSKI LOOP, TOO

CANNON BEACH TO ECOLA STATE PARK

ST. HELENS

SAUVIE ISLAND JOURNEY

ALONG THE MIAMI RIVER TO NEHALEM BAY

WASHINGTON

Columbia River

OREGON

HOOD RIVER

TILLAMOOK

THREE CAPES SCENIC ROUTE

ROADS TO CHURCHES AND VINEYARDS

FOREST GROVE

PORTLAND

Following the Nestucca River to the coast

BEAVER

OREGON CITY ROUNDABOUT TO CANBY

CANBY

MEANDERING THROUGH THE WILLAMETTE VALLEY

McMINNVILLE

GRAND ISLAND TOUR

THE SCENIC DRIVE NEAR NESKOWIN

SALEM

THE ROAD TO SILVER CREEK FALLS

RIPPLEBROOK TO TIMOTHY LAKE

A HOT SPRINGS TRIP

THE ROAD TO OLALLIE LAKE

TYGH VALLEY TO SHERAR'S BRIDGE AND MAUPIN

THE ROAD TO WAPINITIA

BAKEOVEN TO SHANIKO

SHANIKO

SMITH FIELD SLOUGH

ELK CITY TO NEWPORT

FALLS CITY AND BASKETT

RURAL ROUTE TO SALEM

FALLS CITY TO FALLS

THE ROAD TO KINGS VALLEY

ALONG THE SILETZ RIVER

HOSKINS

NEWPORT

THE ROAD TO ELK CITY

ALBANY

CORVALLIS

ANTELOPE AND THE ROAD TO ASHWOOD

MADRAS

FROM BILLY CHINOOK TO WIZARD FALLS AND THE HEAD OF THE METOLIUS

THE ROAD PAST STEIN'S PILLAR

PRINEVILLE

ALSEA

THE ROAD TO ALSEA FALLS

MONROE

PEORIA ROAD AND BEYOND

ROADS AROUND AND ABOUT BROWNSVILLE

SISTERS

BACK ROAD ONGST

AM THE BLUFFS

REDMOND

FOLLOWING THE CROOKED RIVER

THE OLD TERRITORIAL ROAD

Northwestern Oregon

EUGENE

BEND

ANLAUF

Pacific Ocean

Northwestern Oregon

Foxglove

Northwestern Oregon

This is a land of enchanting Pacific shoreline, lush green coastal forest, great snowcapped inland mountains, majestic rivers and fertile valleys, and high desert land textured with sagebrush and juniper.

The old Territorial Road

You can travel the old stage road from Anlauf north to Monroe. Along Pheasant Creek, it twists and turns as the original road probably did long ago. Farther north it has been smoothed and straightened into a fast highway.

Near Franklin I sketched the Allen barn, erected in 1900, two years before the house was built. A chipmunk sat gnawing an acorn just a few yards from my feet. I included it in the picture.

The Allen barn, 1900

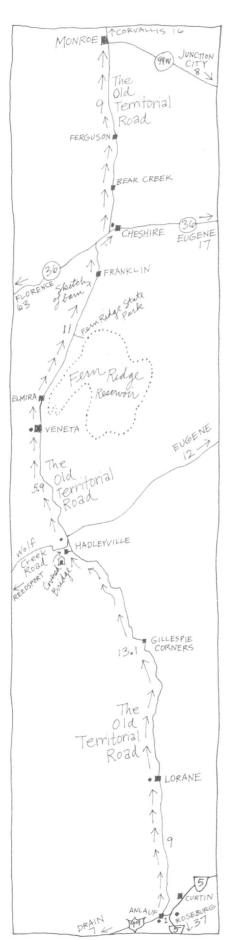

MONROE ↑CORVALLIS 16
(99W) JUNCTION CITY 8 →
The Old Territorial Road
9
FERGUSON
BEAR CREEK
(36) →
CHESHIRE EUGENE 17
(36)
FLORENCE 63
FRANKLIN
Sketch of barn
Fern Ridge State Park
11
Fern Ridge Reservoir
ELMIRA
VENETA
EUGENE 12 →
The Old Territorial Road
5.9
Wolf Creek Road
REEDSPORT
Covered Bridge
HADLEYVILLE
GILLESPIE CORNERS
13.1
The Old Territorial Road
LORANE
9
(5)
CURTIN
ANLAUF
DRAIN (99) 1 ROSEBURG 37
(5) ↓37

AIR MAIL

EVERIT LAVE
HAW
H—

90

Back road airmail

Back road
mailbox

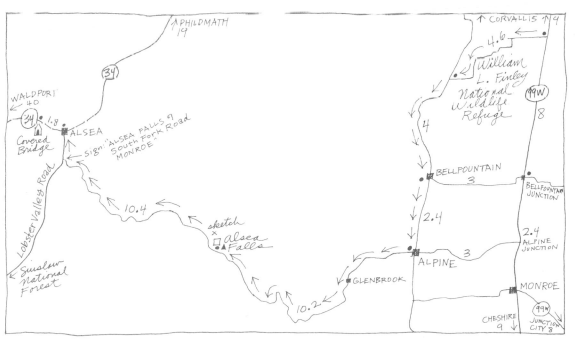

Alsea Falls

*The road to
Alsea Falls*

South of Corvallis off Highway 99W this back road
begins at the William L. Finley National Wildlife Refuge.
This is farming country, then farther on near the falls,
forested land. I camped at Alsea Falls and woke next
morning to the sounds and sight of a squirrel chewing a
green fir cone to bits. While sketching the falls early
that day, I saw thousands of caterpillars inching
their way over the rocks next to the Alsea River.
I had to be careful where I stepped.

Buena Vista Ferry

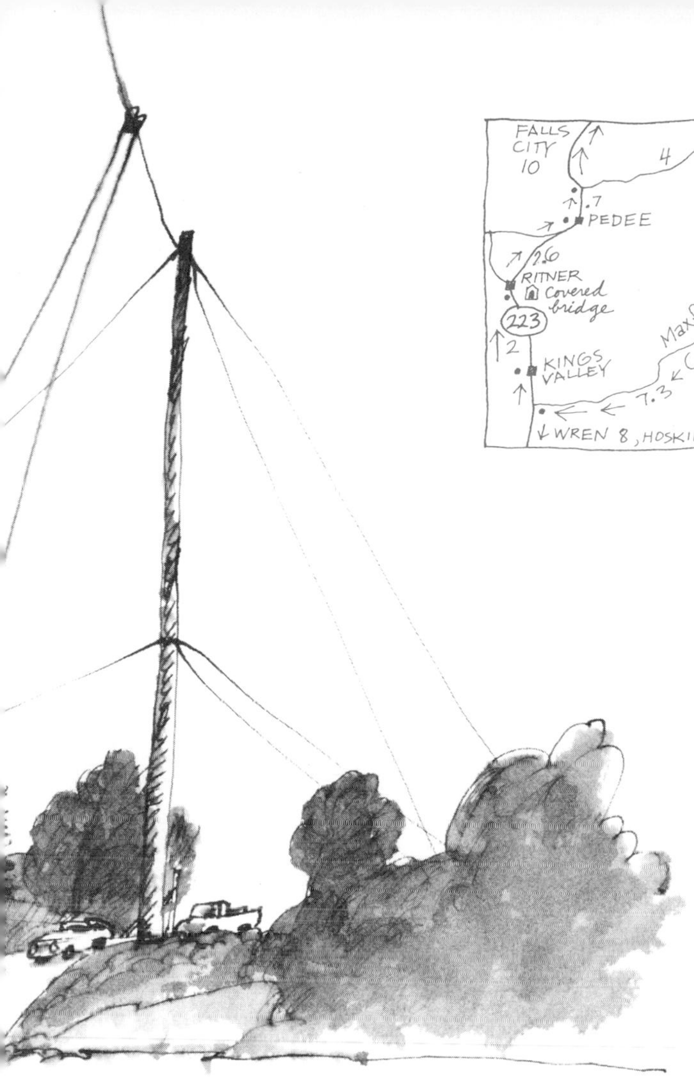

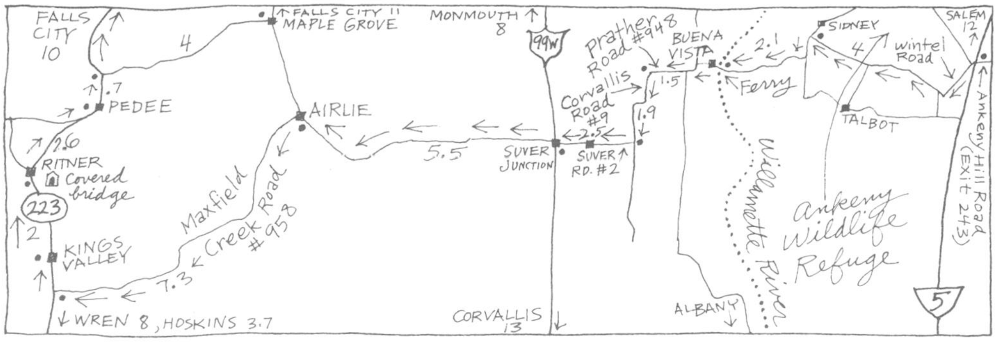
FALLS CITY 10
FALLS CITY 11
MAPLE GROVE
MONMOUTH 8
99W
Prather Road #948
BUENA VISTA
2.1
SIDNEY
4
Wintel Road
SALEM 12
PEDEE
AIRLIE
Corvallis Road #9
1.5
Ferry
1.9
2.5
SUVER JUNCTION
SUVER RD. #2
5.5
RITNER
Covered bridge
223
2
Maxfield Creek Road #958
KINGS VALLEY
7.3
TALBOT
Willamette River
Ankeny Wildlife Refuge
Ankeny Hill Road (Exit 243)
5
WREN 8, HOSKINS 3.7
CORVALLIS 13
ALBANY

Road to Kings Valley

Crops of corn, wheat, hops, bush beans, and mint enrich the scenery on the road to Buena Vista.

A cool crossing of the Willamette on the busy ferry begins a pleasant trip to Airlie and Kings Valley.

To Falls City and Baskett Slough Wildlife Refuge

At the falls a red-haired, freckle-faced boy climbed the waterfall, made a sensational leap clear of the massive rock cliffs to the water below, then scaled the thirty feet of rock cliff to receive my congratulations.

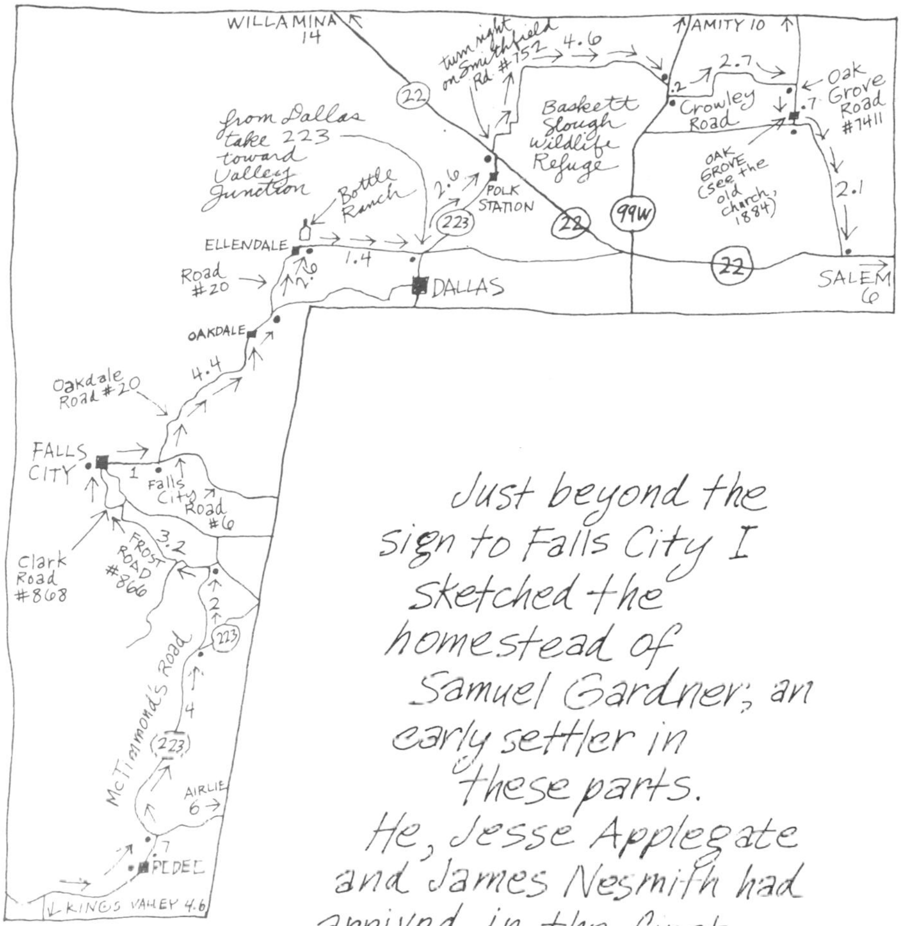
WILLAMINA 14
AMITY 10
turn right on Smithfield Rd #752
4.6
2.7
Oak Grove Road #7411
Baskett Slough Wildlife Refuge
Crowley Road
from Dallas take 223 toward Valley Junction
Bottle Ranch
POLK STATION
OAK GROVE (see the old church, 1884)
2.1
2.6
ELLENDALE
1.4
Road #20
DALLAS
SALEM 6
OAKDALE
Oakdale Road #20
4.4
FALLS CITY
Falls City Road #6
Clark Road #868
FROST ROAD #866
3.2
McTimmond's Road
AIRLIE 6
PEDEE
KINGS VALLEY 4.6

Just beyond the sign to Falls City I sketched the homestead of Samuel Gardner, an early settler in these parts. He, Jesse Applegate and James Nesmith had arrived in the first wagon train to Polk County in 1843.

Not far beyond the hamlet of Ellendale was Bottle Ranch, adorned with astonishing bottle motifs.

Dallas has an interesting block of historic buildings along its main square.

Samuel Gardner Homestead

The road to Elk City

Elk City is a quiet hamlet along the Yaquina River. You can buy worms at the store and sit on the pier to fish the quiet river.

Inspired by Elk City's restfulness, I camped near the store under a great Oregon ash tree where there once had been a sawmill.

I awoke in the morning to find a huge local setter pointing directly at me; I guess a stranger in town was not necessarily to be trusted. We made friends, however.

Elk City store

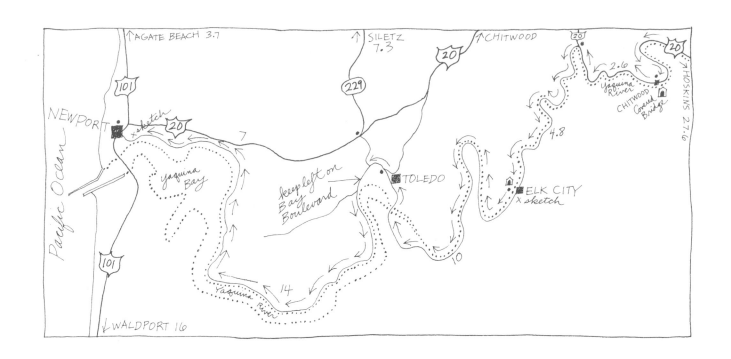

The map shows the route from Elk City to Newport following the Yaquina. Labels include:

↑ AGATE BEACH 3.7

↑ SILETZ 7.3

↑ CHITWOOD

101

NEWPORT

× sketch

Pacific Ocean

20

229

20

2.6

Yaquina River

CHITWOOD Covered Bridge

↗ HOSKINS 27.6

7

Yaquina Bay

keep left on Bay Boulevard

TOLEDO

4.8

ELK CITY
× sketch

10

14

Yaquina River

101

↓ WALDPORT 16

Elk City to Newport following the Yaquina

The road hugged the shore of the river.
Mist rose from its surface in the early morning.
Hundreds of fishing boats of all kinds were
moored or beached near Newport, and fish
and shellfish could be purchased at a
lively wharf area.

Yaquina Bay fishing boat

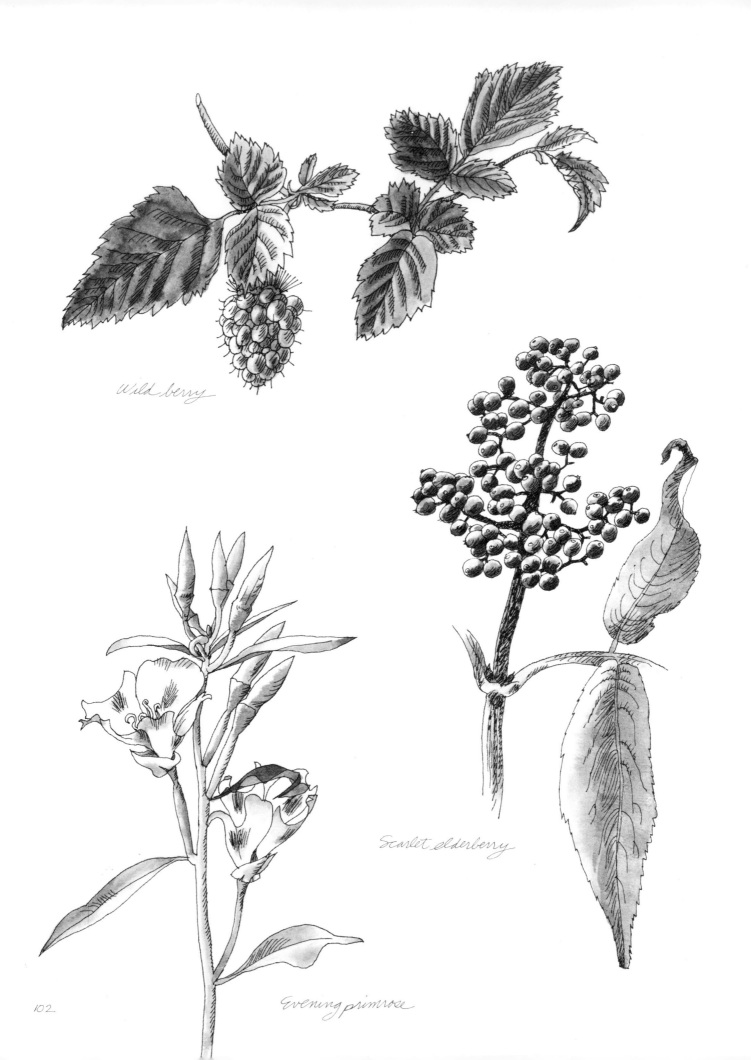

Wild berry

Scarlet elderberry

Evening primrose

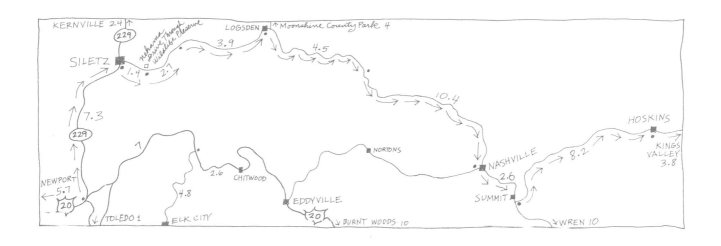

KERNVILLE 24 ↑
229
Nakama Drive Through Wildlife Preserve
LOGSDEN ← Moonshine County Park 4
3.9
4.5
SILETZ
1.4   2.7
10.4
HOSKINS
7.3
229
KINGS VALLEY 3.8
NEWPORT
5.7
20
2.6   CHITWOOD
NORTONS
NASHVILLE
8.2
2.6
EDDYVILLE
SUMMIT
4.8
20
↓ TOLEDO 1   ELK CITY   ↓ BURNT WOODS 10   ↓ WREN 10

Along the Siletz River to old Fort Hoskins

On this trip there were meadows and barns and forest as well as a drive through a wildlife preserve. Wild flowers were a continual joy to discover as I sketched.

Back road ruminants

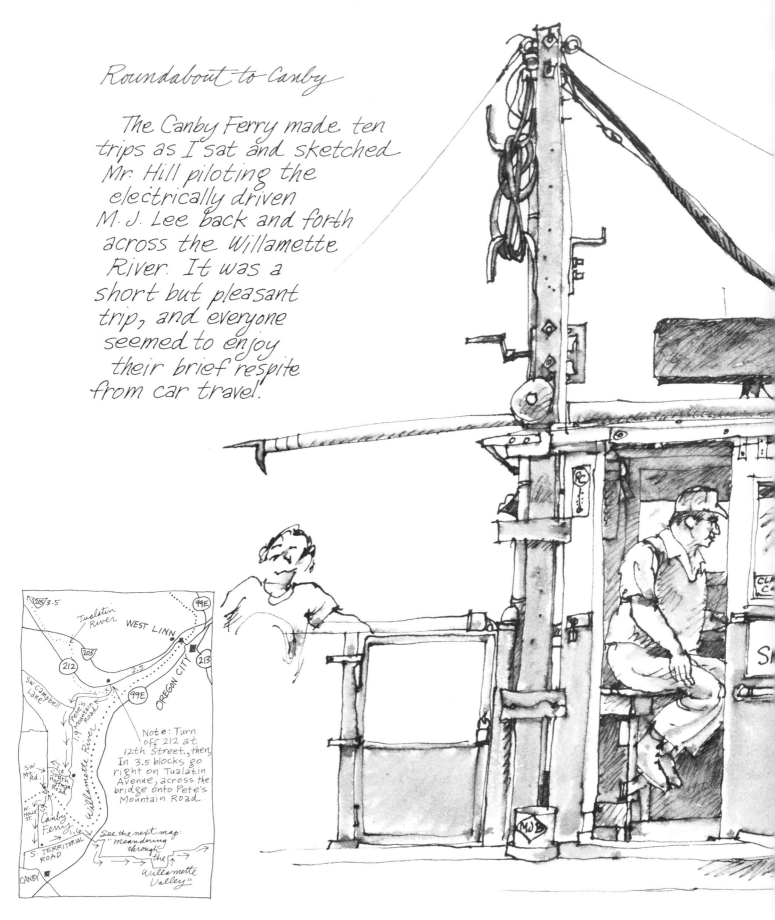

Roundabout to Canby

The Canby Ferry made ten trips as I sat and sketched Mr. Hill piloting the electrically driven M. J. Lee back and forth across the Willamette River. It was a short but pleasant trip, and everyone seemed to enjoy their brief respite from car travel.

Note: Turn off 212 at 12th Street, then, in 3.5 blocks go right on Tualatin Avenue, across the bridge onto Pete's Mountain Road

See the next map: "Meandering through the Willamette Valley"

Canby Ferry

FREE

LIFE PRESERVERS
IN CABIN

EFC 280
MℓOREGON

Canby Ferry ↑ 1.9 → 1.6 → East Territorial Road .6 ↑OREGON CITY 6 ← South Beaver Creek Road ↑FISCHERS MILL
S. Territorial Road ← South Haines Road .6
1.6 South Carus Road 3.4 CARUS ← 2.8 → 1.7 ← 5
South Bremer Road (views of Mt. Hood) South Central Point Road .2 Sign: "S LWR HIGHLD RD."
BARLOW 99E
AURORA 2
LONE ELDER
S. Lewellen Rd. HIGHLAND
1.8 .6
CLARKES FOUR CORNERS South Meyers Road S. Lewellen Road
MULINO 1.9
213 South Unger Road ×sketch of Kloeri bam
UNION MILLS 2 Windy City Road 3.8 1.2 ←
Rock Creek Church South Beaver Creek Road
1.8 Sconce Road
Smyrna Church ↓ Gordon Road ← MEADOWBROOK 211 ESTACADA
↓ 2.7 COLTON OLD COLTON
S. Dryland Road CEDARDALE
HAMRICKS CORNER 1.5 2.1 ← S. Cochran Road MOLALLA
South Barlow Road 2.9 YODER South Schneider Road 1.5 Feyrer County Park
Darnell-Gibson Road
1.3 .3 213
South Eagan Road KOKEL CORNER ↓
South Thompson Road South Kropf Rd. SCOTTS MILLS ↓
South Lee Road MARQUAM ↓To Scotts Mills

Note: In all practicality I could not include all of the many roads in this area of the Willamette Valley. Please refer to a Marion County map for complete details. This is an accurate account of my trip, however.

106

Meandering through the Willamette Valley

The road went through farm and forest land with a stop to sketch at the Kloer ranch, where sheep grazed among the stumps.

The Kloer ranch

At Yoder the amiable Walters family ran the
neatly kept old store. The store was purchased
by Paul and Audrey Yoder in 1990. They painted
it red, so its appearance is somewhat
altered from this, my original drawing.
   Not far from here is the 1857 Rock Creek
Church set in a historic cemetery. The church
is still in use for special occasions.

Old Yoder Store
run by Walters family,
early 1980s

North Falls

The road to Silver Creek Falls

There are ten falls to see if you hike on all the trails at Silver Creek Falls State Park. One-hundred-thirty-six-foot North Falls is easy to reach via a short trail. One can actually walk around and under the falls to more fully experience its magnificence.

The road to Olallie Lake

This was a rough-surfaced road through high mountain scenery to Olallie Lake. The lake was calm. Voices could be heard clearly for long distances across the water. Mt. Jefferson seemed a bit unreal, like a painted backdrop for a stage setting.

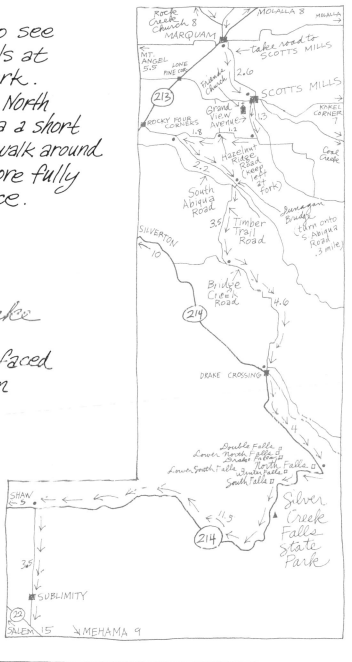

Olallie Lake and Mount Jefferson

a hot springs trip

There were hot springs at
Breitenbush, at Austin, and at Bagby.
A one-and-one-half-mile trail took me to
Bagby Hot Springs. Through the
courtesy of Mt. Hood National Forestry
Service, there were five separate rooms
available for the natural hot baths.
Steaming water welled up from the
bowels of the earth and flowed past the
open window. I pulled the trough
bung to fill my big cedar tub, then
brought buckets of cold water from
the creek to dilute the very hot
spring water.

While I soaked in the log tub,
thunder rolled and crashed over the
Cascades and rain drummed on the
roof of the rustic bathhouse—
and I didn't care.

Bagby Hot Springs

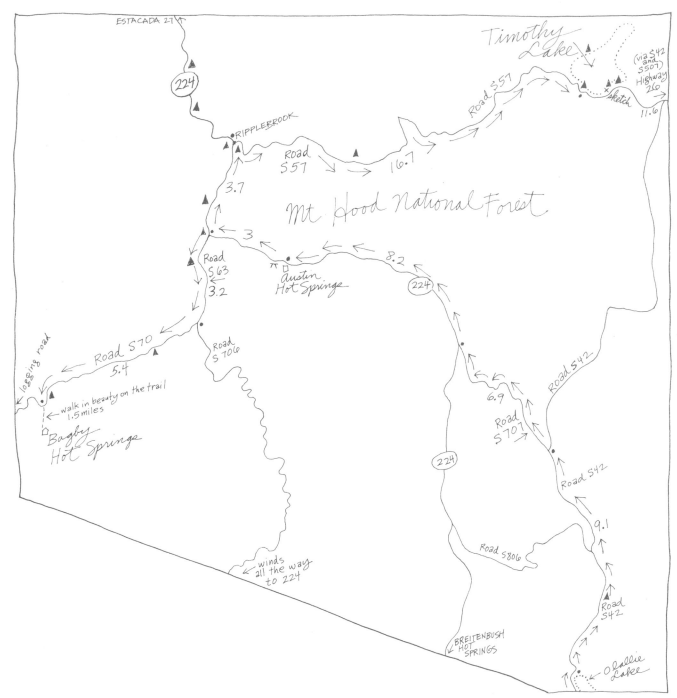

ESTACADA 27
224
RIPPLEBROOK
Road S57
Road S57
3.7
16.7

Timothy Lake
(via S42 and S507)
Highway 26
11.6
sketch

Mt. Hood National Forest

3
Road S63
3.2
Austin Hot Springs
8.2
224

logging road
Road S70
5.4
Road S706
walk in beauty on the trail 1.5 miles
Bagby Hot Springs

winds all the way to 224

224
224

6.9
Road S701
Road S42

Road S42

9.1
Road S806

Road S42

BREITENBUSH HOT SPRINGS

Olallie Lake

Ripplebrook to Timothy Lake

Mount Hood is a graceful backdrop
for Timothy Lake.   Motorboats
are easily launched on the
lake, which is a popular spot
for families and fishermen.

116

The road to Wapinitia, Wamic, and Tygh Valley

This is great volcanic plateau land, made even more dramatic by occasional gorges that cut across great areas of landscape.

There was thunder and lightning in the distance and threatening rainclouds gathering overhead. It was 7PM, and a farmer I passed was desperately threshing the wheat in his fields to get it in before the deluge.

Earlier I sat on Lloyd and Dixie Woodside's porch in Wapinitia and drew at least one-half of the town, with Mount Hood in the background.

Wapinitia was a much larger town in the days when wagoneers hauled freight between The Dalles and Prineville. That traffic ended many years ago, when the new railroad took over the job.

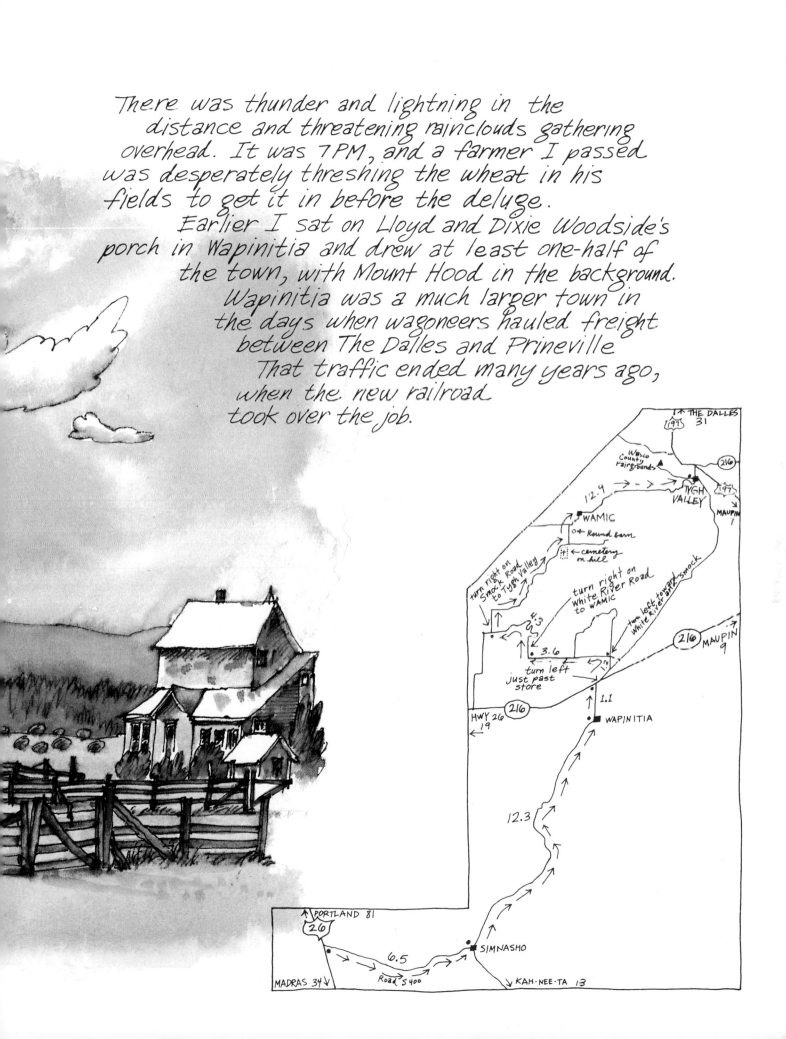

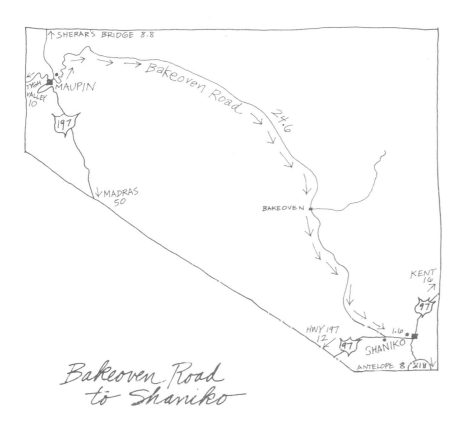

Bakeoven Road
to Shaniko

    I don't think the look of
the hotel at Shaniko has changed a great
deal since its beginnings. Once called the
Columbia Southern Hotel, in 1902 the
Shaniko Leader had this to say about it...
"This house is a large two-story brick structure,
finished throughout with the very best of
everything, and is one of the leading hotels
in eastern Oregon. On both floors will be
found hot and cold water, toilet rooms,
bathtubs, etc. It has a fine sewer
connection and no refuse or offensive
matter can pervade the atmosphere, as
is too often noticeable in hotels, especially
in the interior."

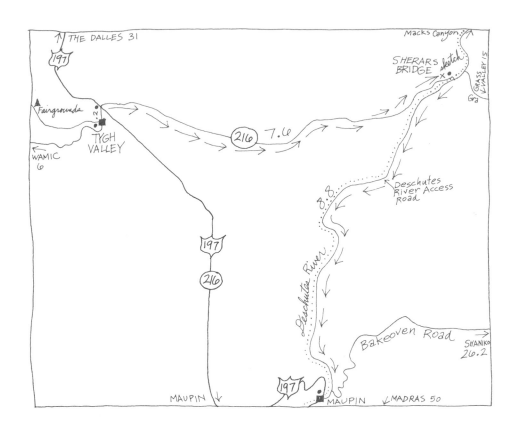

Indians salmon fishing on the Deschutes River

Tygh Valley to Sherars Bridge and Maupin

Near Sherars Bridge the ancient Indian trail
led to a place where the rushing Deschutes River
could be forded. The earliest pioneers floated
their wagons across this stretch.

Indians were fishing here the day I sketched.
They tended great nets amid the pounding turmoil
and spray of the river at its frothiest point.

Antelope Community Church

Antelope and the road to Ashwood

Antelope seemed a peaceful place.
I sketched the well-preserved Antelope
Community Church to the musical accompaniment
of lawn sprinklers, a crowing rooster, and the
rustling of cottonwood tree leaves overhead.

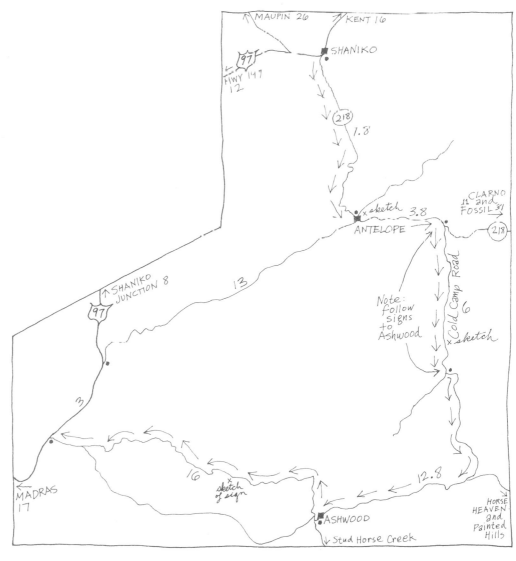

Road to Ashwood

The store at Ashwood is half-grocery and
half-rock shop, for this is agate and thunderegg
country. A thunderegg is a rock that is shaped
very roughly like an egg. One must slice it,
however, to see the interesting interior pattern.

At her ranch near Ashwood Mrs. Swanson told me that the sign along the road for attracting rock collectors used to read "Eggs and Agate." Since she has changed the sign to "Agate and Eggs" people do not ask for chicken eggs any longer.

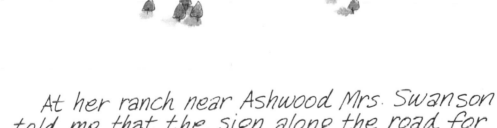

SWANSON AGATE & EGGS PRESENTS:

CHIEF PAULINA REDS.

VARIETY GOLDS.

BROWNS & BLUES

WITH PLUME, PRETZEL POLKA-DOT + TUBE DESIGN →

OPEN

The air smelled sweet with growing mint around
Madras. I sketched the bluffs at Lake Billy
Chinook to a chorus of doves in the cliffs in back
of me. The road around the lake winds through
rock and juniper.
      At Wizard Falls you will notice the especially
clear quality of the water of the Metolius
River. I sketched a yellow monkey flower
      along the bank while listening to the
      rushing sound of these purest of waters.
            The fish hatchery here is one
            of Oregon's most parklike and
                  was a great
                        pleasure
                        to visit.

Bluffs above Lake Billy Chinook

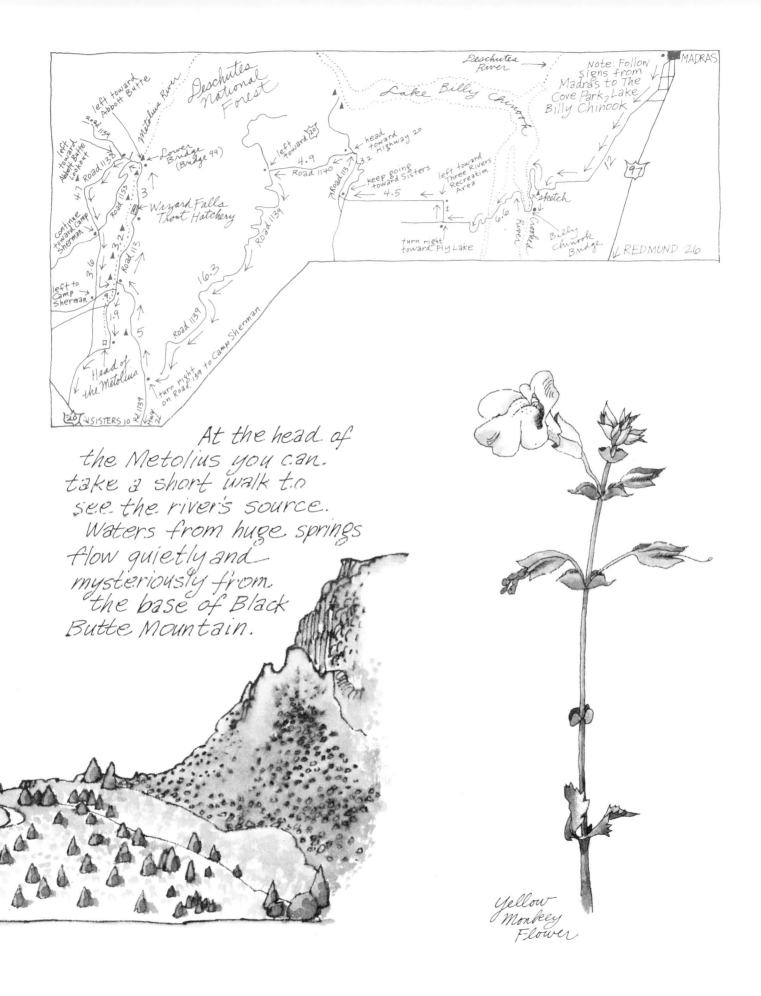

Map Labels

Deschutes National Forest

Metolius River

Deschutes River

Lake Billy Chinook

MADRAS

Note: Follow signs from Madras to The Cove Park, Lake Billy Chinook

left toward Abbott Butte

Road 1154

left toward Abbott Butte Lookout

Road 1130

Lower Bridge (Bridge 99)

left toward 20

4.9

Road 1140

head toward Highway 20

keep going toward Sisters

4.5

Road 113

3.2

left toward Three Rivers Recreation Area

Road 1153

3

Wizard Falls Trout Hatchery

Road 113

Continue toward camp Sherman

4.7

3.6

3.2

Road 113

Road 1139

16.3

Road 1139

left to Camp Sherman

4.2

1.9

5

turn right toward Fly Lake

1

6.6

Crooked River

sketch

Billy Chinook Bridge

97

12

REDMOND 26

Head of the Metolius

turn right on Road 1139 to Camp Sherman

Road 1139

20

SISTERS 10

Hwy 22

At the head of
the Metolius you can
take a short walk to
see the river's source.
Waters from huge springs
flow quietly and
mysteriously from
the base of Black
Butte Mountain.

Yellow
Monkey
Flower

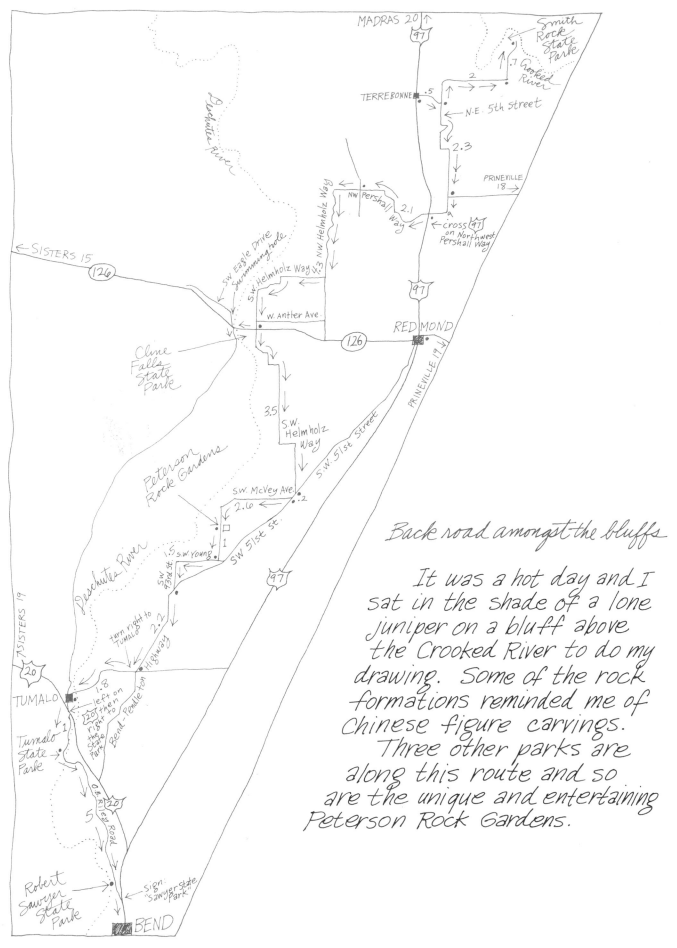

MADRAS 20 ↑
97

Smith Rock State Park

.7 Crooked River

2

TERREBONNE .5

N.E. 5th street

2.3

PRINEVILLE 18 →

NW Pershall Way

2.1

cross 97 on Northwest Pershall Way

NW Helmholz Way

← SISTERS 15
126

SW Eagle Drive swimming hole

SW Helmholz Way 4.3

W. Antler Ave.

97

RED MOND
126

Cline Falls State Park

PRINEVILLE 19

3.5

S.W. Helmholz Way

S.W. 51st Street

Peterson Rock Gardens

Deschutes River

SW. McVey Ave.
2.6   .2

1

SW 51st St.

.5 s.w. young

SW 93rd St.

SW 51st St.

97

↑ SISTERS 19

Turn right to TUMALO

2.2

Bend-Pendleton Highway

20

TUMALO

.8
left on 20 then right to the state park

1 ← Tumalo State Park

O.B. Riley Road

20

5

Robert Sawyer State Park

Sign "Sawyer state park"

BEND

Back road amongst the bluffs

It was a hot day and I sat in the shade of a lone Juniper on a bluff above the Crooked River to do my drawing. Some of the rock formations reminded me of Chinese figure carvings.
Three other parks are along this route and so are the unique and entertaining Peterson Rock Gardens.

Smith Rock

Steins Pillar

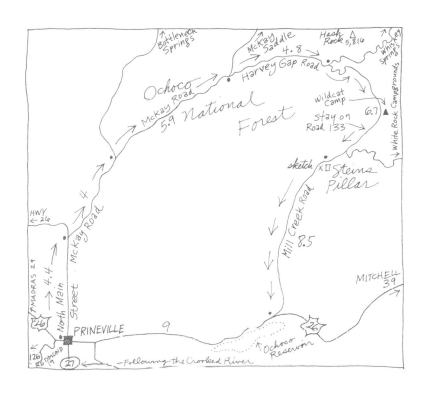

The map shows (as labels):

Bottleneck Springs
McKay Saddle 4.8
Hash Rock 5,816
Whisky Springs
Ochoco McKay Road
5.9 National Forest
Harvey Gap Road
Wildcat Camp
stay on Road 133
6.7
White Rock Campgrounds
sketch X□ Steins Pillar
McKay Road
HWY ← 26
MADRAS 29 4.4
North Main Street McKay Road
Mill Creek Road 8.5
MITCHELL 39
26
PRINEVILLE 9
26
126 REDMOND 19
27
— Following the Crooked River
↗ Ochoco Reservoir

The road past Steins Pillar

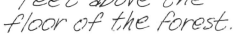

The valley drive past farms and crops soon
became forest. On the return journey
there was a clear view of
Steins Pillar, a geological
oddity towering 350
feet above the
floor of the forest.

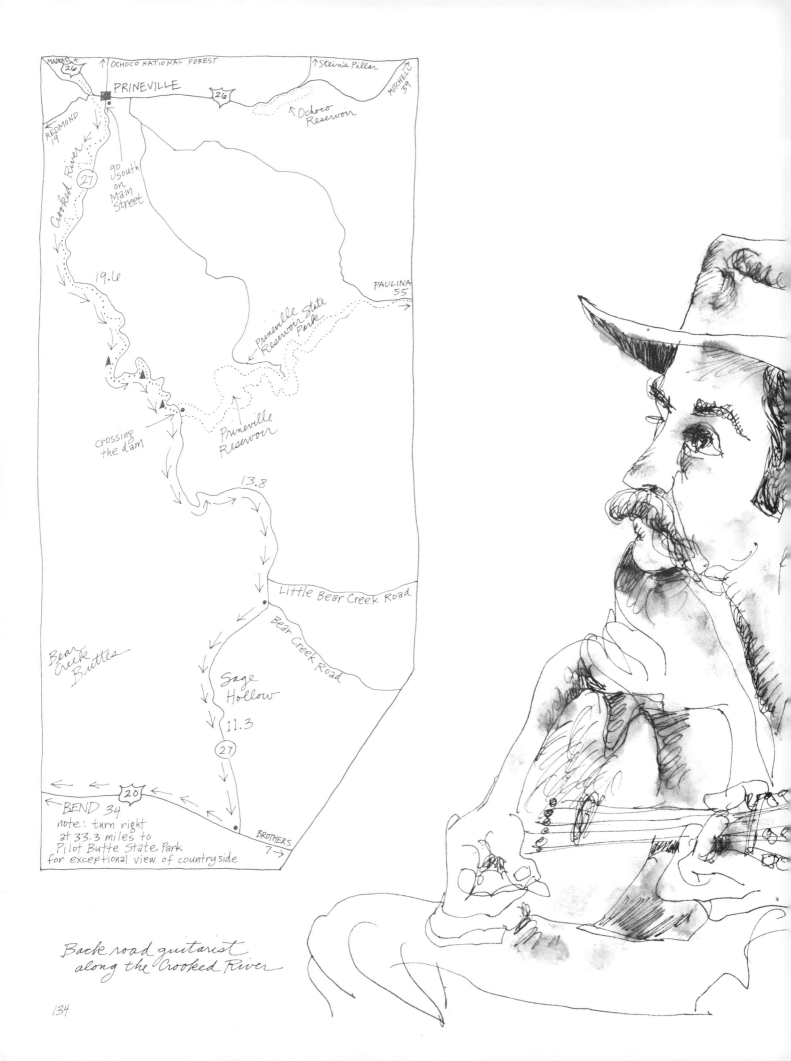

MADRAS 26

↑ OCHOCO NATIONAL FOREST

↑ Stein's Pillar

PRINEVILLE

26

MITCHELL 39

REDMOND 19

↑ Ochoco Reservoir

Crooked River

27

go south on Main Street

19.6

PAULINA 55

Prineville State Reservoir Park

Prineville Reservoir

crossing the dam

13.8

Little Bear Creek Road

Bear Creek Buttes

Bear Creek Road

Sage Hollow

11.3

27

20

BEND 34
note: turn right
at 33.3 miles to
Pilot Butte State Park
for exceptional view of countryside

BROTHERS 7 →

Back road guitarist
along the Crooked River

Following the Crooked River

Juniper berries were ripening on all the trees in late August. I rubbed the white bloom from a berry to see its rich dark blue color.

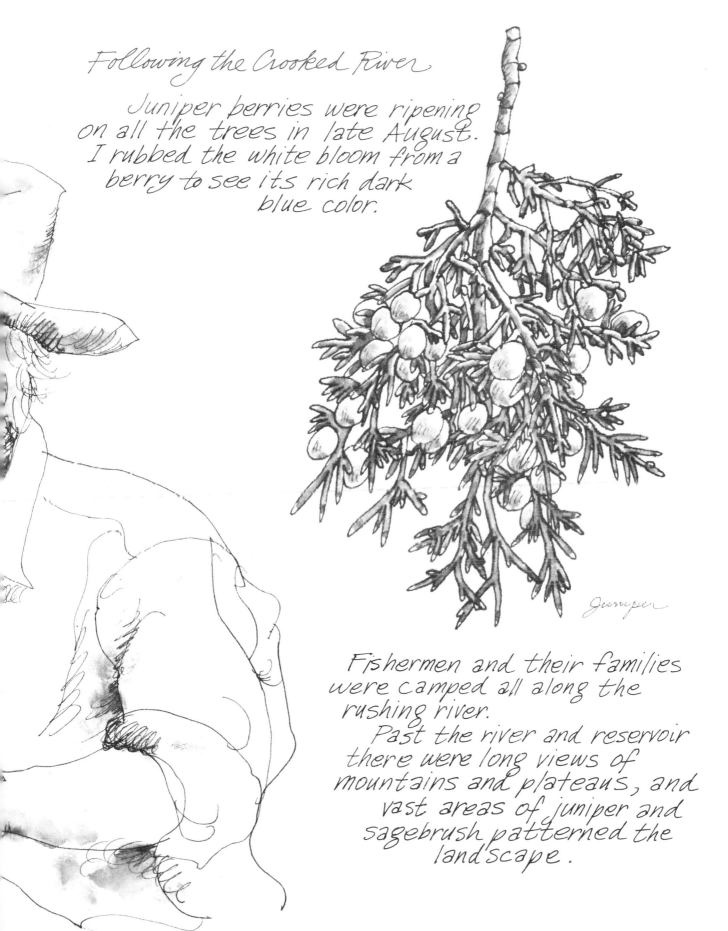

Juniper

Fishermen and their families were camped all along the rushing river.

Past the river and reservoir there were long views of mountains and plateaus, and vast areas of juniper and sagebrush patterned the landscape.

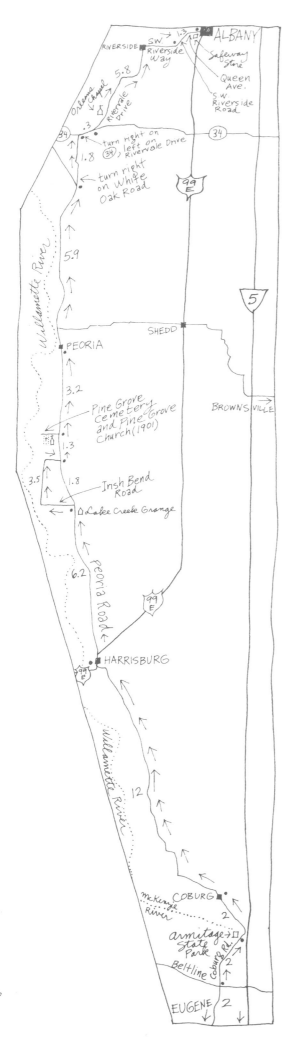

Peoria Road and beyond

This road followed the east bank of the Willamette River past well-kept farms and sweet-smelling fields of mint and clover.

I stopped at the Pine Grove Community Church south of Peoria to sketch. One of the donors of the land where the church and cemetery stand was William Shepard. His baby son had been placed in the first grave there in 1853.

Pine Grove Community Church.

Roads around and about Brownsville

I sat in the shade of a tree that was heavily decorated with pears to sketch the Blair Hop-curing House. Along with other historic buildings in Brownsville (such as the well-restored Moyer House), it gave me a feeling for times past.

Blair Hop-curing House

This trip meanders along the Calapooia River, offering views of farms and forest landscapes, and opportunities to explore out-of-the-way places.
In Brownsville, where residents sit on their front porches of a pleasant evening, there must have been mild speculation as to who was this tourist driving slowly down their street. It would have been better to walk. Then there is more of a chance for a friendly greeting.

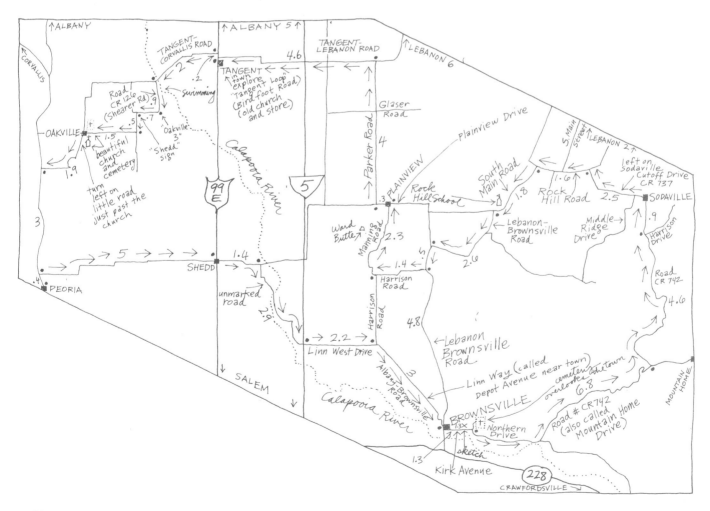

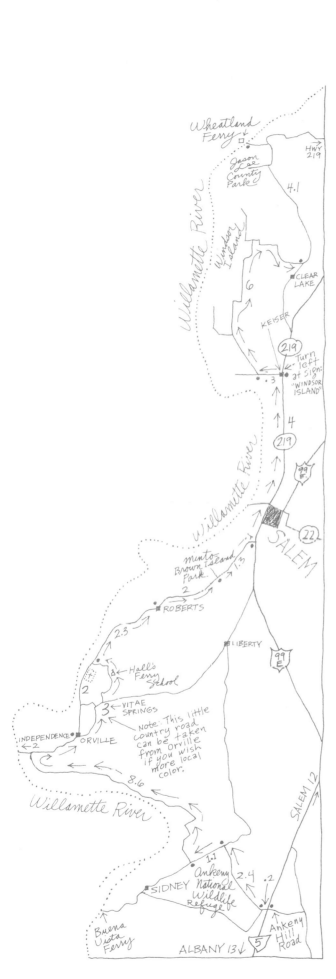

Hops

Rural route to Salem and
the Wheatland Ferry

Still following the Willamette
north, I was entertained by
the view of fertile farm
country and the smell of
freshly cut crops. Once I
stopped to admire fields of
decorative, twining hop vines.
I sketched some of the
green hop cones and leaves.
Ripened and dried, these
cones impart a pleasant,
somewhat bitter flavor to
malt liquors.

UNIONVALE

DAYTON
6.6

McMINNVILLE

14

GRAND
ISLAND
JUNCTION

1.3

FOUR
CORNERS

2

221 2.2

X sketch
Grand
Island

3.8

Willamette River

PINE
TREE
CORNER

HOPEWELL

Maud
Williamson
State Park

1.1

WHEATLAND

Wheatland
Ferry

SALEM 12

Smitty's Produce,
Grand Island

Grand Island tour

There were so many sprinklers going
as I drove along one stretch of this
bucolic farm road around Grand Island
that I needed to keep my windshield
wipers working and windows closed.
At Smitty's roadside vegetable
stand, Snoopy, the dog, ate
a large portion of yellow
wax stringbeans as
I sketched. Here's
hoping Smitty's
is still there.

U-PICK
OPEN
U-Pick
BEANS
PICKLES

BEANS
ONIONS
TODAY
OPEN

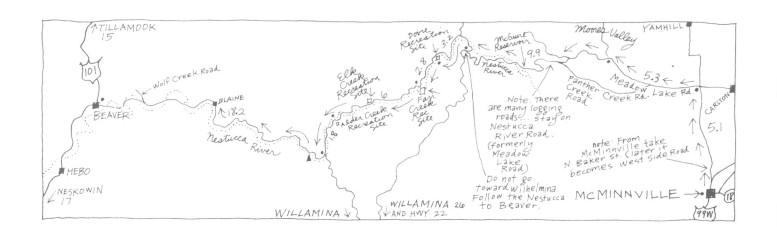

Following the Nestucca River to the coast

Leaving the Carlton area there were long
views of valleys and farms and big barns.
Past the grand panorama of Moore's
Valley I headed for the green forests
of the Siuslaw National Forest.
The road along the Nestucca River
led to the town of Beaver.

Cows and redwood tree stumps near Beaver

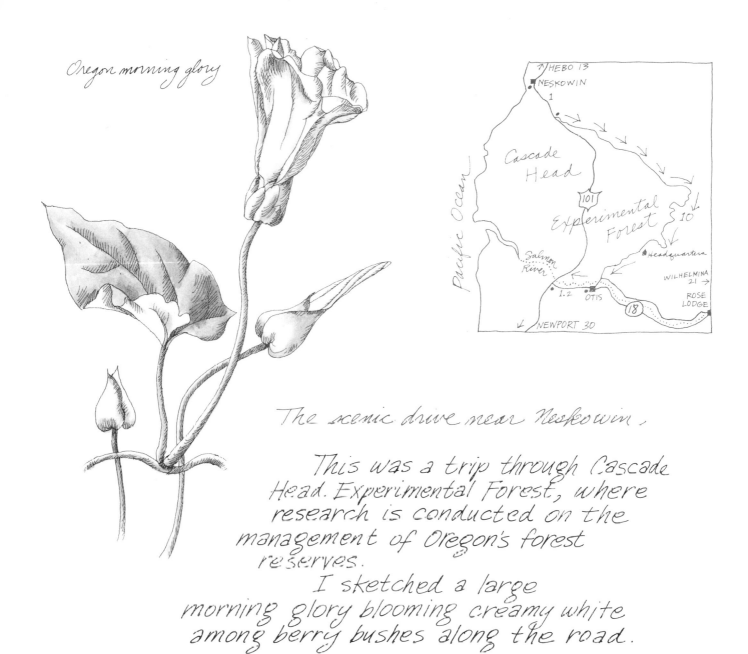

Oregon morning glory

The scenic drive near Neskowin.

This was a trip through Cascade Head Experimental Forest, where research is conducted on the management of Oregon's forest reserves.

I sketched a large morning glory blooming creamy white among berry bushes along the road.

Three Capes scenic route

At Cape Kiwanda dories on boat trailers awaited their silver-salmon-fishing owners in a storage lot near the beach. Some trailers had rusty old trucks and cars attached to them ready to go, that is, if the aged vehicles could be started. The dories are flat bottomed and are launched from the beach at Kiwanda. The one I selected to sketch was named Dumship.

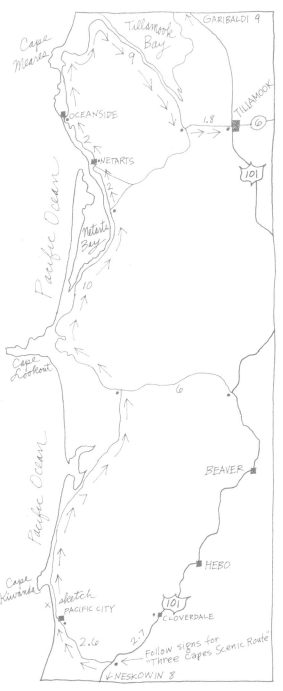

Dumship, Cape Kiwanda

The entire trip was a delight of grand coastal scenery. As I rounded the shores of Tillamook Bay herons were poised in the shallow water, prepared to select any fishy bit that might venture by.

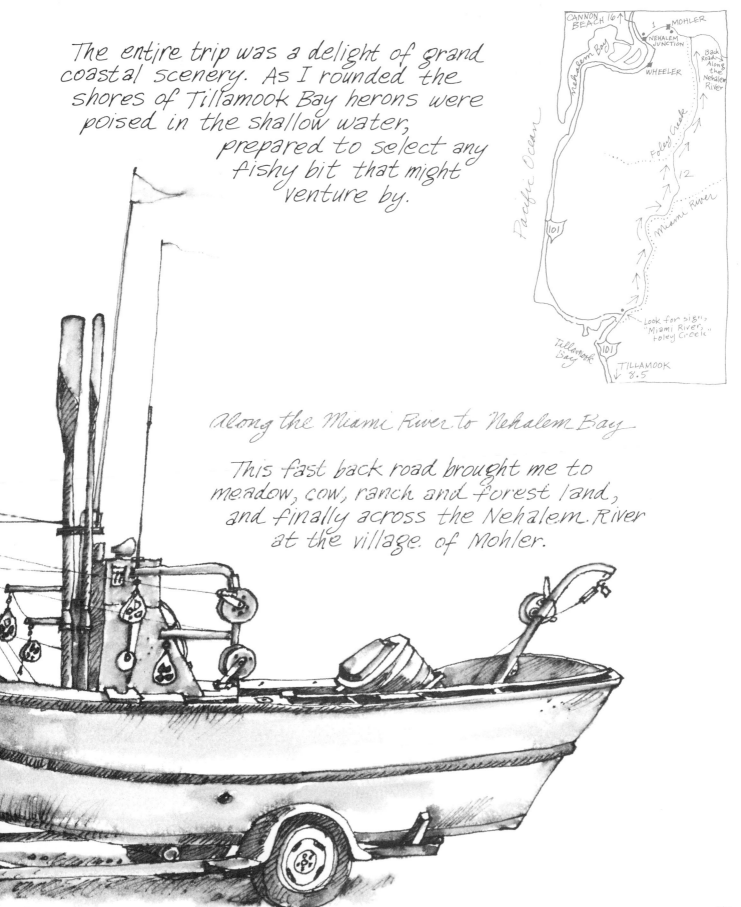

Along the Miami River to Nehalem Bay

This fast back road brought me to meadow, cow, ranch and forest land, and finally across the Nehalem River at the village of Mohler.

147

Cannon Beach to
Ecola State Park

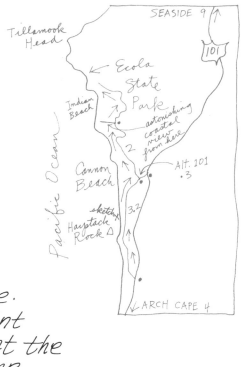

I was at work sketching
very early in the morning.
Birds flocked around
Haystack Rock, their cries
mingling with the sound of the
ocean waves tumbling on the
sand. The scene was
intriguing to both ear and eye.
Later at the overlook point
in Ecola Park I marveled at the
beauty of the Oregon coastline.

Haystack Rock

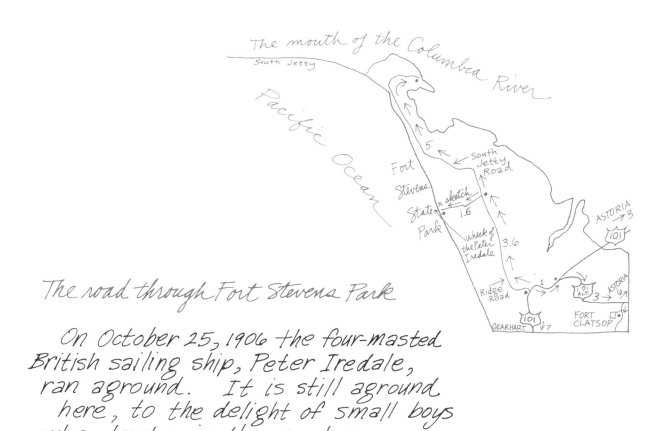

The mouth of the Columbia River

South Jetty

Pacific Ocean

Fort Stevens State Park

South Jetty Road

x sketch 1.6

wreck of the Peter Iredale 3.6

ASTORIA 3

101

Ridge Road

101 ALT. 3

ASTORIA 6

GEARHART

101

FORT CLATSOP

The road through Fort Stevens Park

On October 25, 1906 the four-masted British sailing ship, Peter Iredale, ran aground.   It is still aground here, to the delight of small boys who clamber in the wreckage.
     I drove clear to the end of South Jetty Road for a view of the mouth of the Columbia River and the shoreline of the state of Washington.
     The re-creation of Lewis and Clark's winter headquarters at Fort Clatsop was the next thing to see.

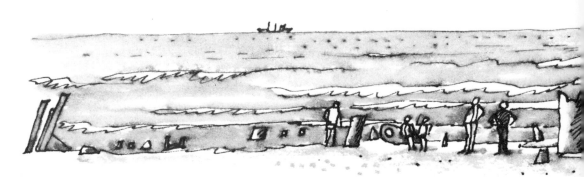

The wreck of the Peter Iredale

Youngs River Loop and Walluski Loop, too

Along Youngs River I made
a picture of an old barn,
now minus its silo, but still
in use and appreciated by
both cows and artists alike.
　　　　I stopped to view
Youngs River Falls. A number
of cars were parked nearby
and I discovered their occupants
swimming and splashing at the
base of the roaring falls.
　　　　The Walluski Loop drive was
a visual feast of farm and barn,
stream and slough.

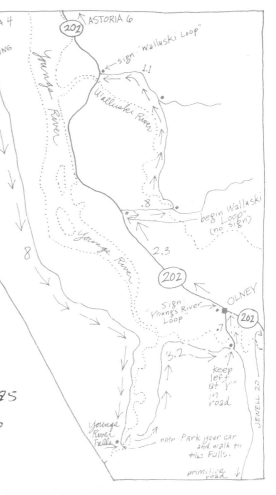

Youngs River

153

Buttercup

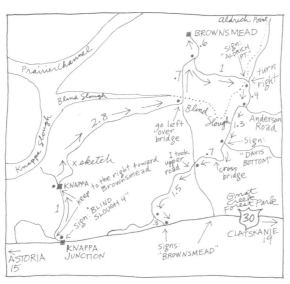

Prairie Channel

Blind Slough

Knappa Slough

2.8 →

x sketch

KNAPPA

1

keep to the right toward
Brownsmead

Sign: "BLIND
SLOUGH 4"

ASTORIA
15

KNAPPA
JUNCTION

signs:
"BROWNSMEAD"

I took
upper
road

1.5

.3

go left
over
bridge

Blind
Slough

.7

cross
bridge

Sign:
"DAVIS
BOTTOM"

1.3

Anderson
Road

mat
Creek
Forest Park

30

CLATSKANIE
19

Aldrich Point

BROWNSMEAD

.6

Sign:
"ALDRICH
PT."

.7

1

.4

turn
right

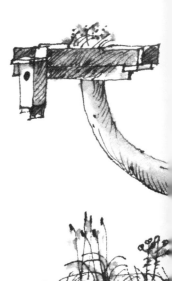

Bob Ziak's sign
near Brownsmead

154

The road to Brownsmead

While I was drawing this scene, Mr. Ziak
came by in his tractor. When he realized I
was sketching his Canadian goose nest,
woodduck house, and sign, he marched, hammer
in hand, to nail up the last part of his message,
which had fallen down. The complete sign then
read, "This land dedicated to the song of birds,
the sound of wings to all of nature's creatures,
for the joy their presence brings. No hunting.
Bob Ziak." It was the gentlest exhortation
not to hunt on private property that I had
ever seen.
     This was a lovely area of waterways
and meadows for me to enjoy.

NOTICE
THIS LAND
DEDICATED TO
THE SONG OF BIRDS
THE SOUND OF WINGS
TO ALL OF NATURES
CREATURES FOR THE JOY

THEIR   BRING

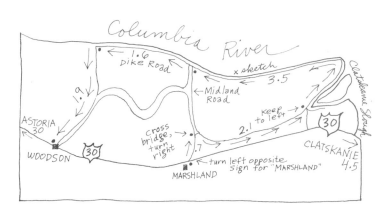

Columbia River

1.6 ← Dike Road →
x sketch 3.5
← Midland Road
keep to left →
2.1 →
cross bridge, turn right
.7
ASTORIA 30
WOODSON 30
.9
Clatskanie Slough
30
CLATSKANIE 4.5
← turn left opposite sign for "MARSHLAND"
MARSHLAND

Levee back road along the Columbia

Trees seem to grow out of old pilings
in the Columbia River. I saw a great
many that day.
    The Columbia River retains its
        majesty even though man has it pretty
    well under control. At several points I had
the feeling I was seeing the great river
    as it was in Lewis and Clark's day, until
an oil tanker would slip around the bend.

The Columbia River

Side road past Mayger on the Columbia

"A man's home is his castle, and so I built mine to look like one," said Tom Flippin.
    Built in the early 1900s it is to this day affectionately referred to as "The Castle."
    Located at 620 Tichenor Street, high on a hill above the little town of Clatskanie, Flippin House National Historic Site, "The Castle," is owned by Clatskanie Senior Citizens and open daily for tours.
    At Mayger Downing Church I ate lunch and inspected headstones in the graveyard.

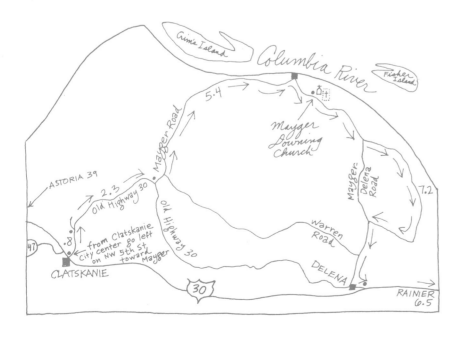

The Flippin House "Castle"

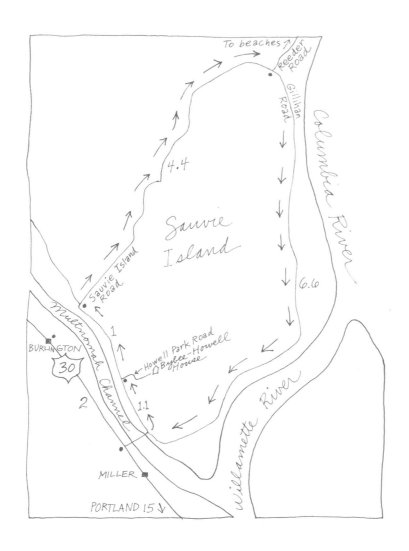

Sauvie Island journey

    I stopped to visit the Bybee-Howell house while traveling around Sauvie Island. It was named after two families that had lived there since it was built in 1856. This historic house is presently maintained by the Oregon Historical Society for Multnomah County and is open to the public. The 1860 doll looking at you in my picture was sitting in a rocking chair in one of the upper rooms.

    I passed many vegetable farms and paused at the popular beaches along the Columbia River.

The doll,
1860

161

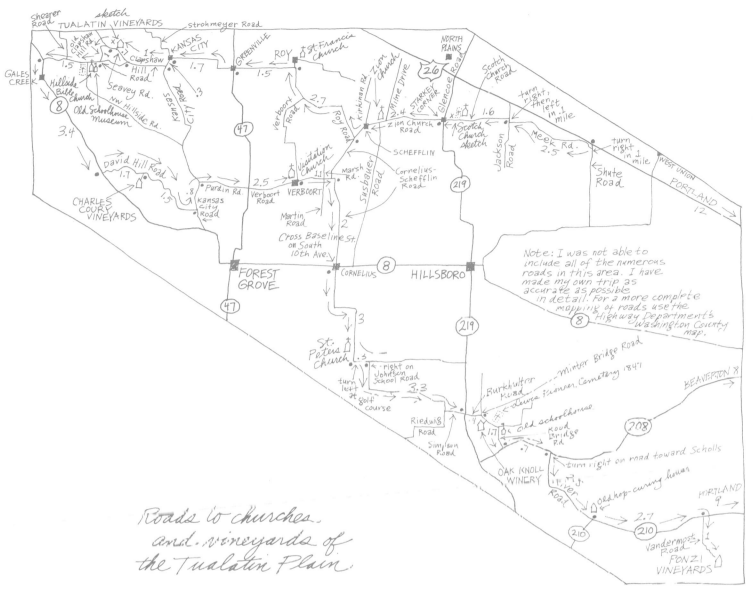

Roads to churches
and vineyards of
the Tualatin Plain.

Certainly one of the most
eye-catching of the Oregon churches
I saw during my travels was
The Old Scotch Church.
I tried to approximate the charm
of its setting of tall trees and
green-lawned cemetery
in this drawing.
At Roy I found another striking
church with a silver tower shining
in the sun.

The Old Scotch Church

164

I tasted one of
winemaker Bill Fuller's
excellent rieslings at Tualatin
Vineyards. To mark the occasion I
sketched this view of a young vineyard
with the Tualatin plain in the distance.
   These back roads took me to four wineries
in all and past views of many fine
churches along the way.
   At the Dutch community of Verboort
the handsome Catholic church was
surrounded by colossal
redwood trees.

Tualatin Vineyards

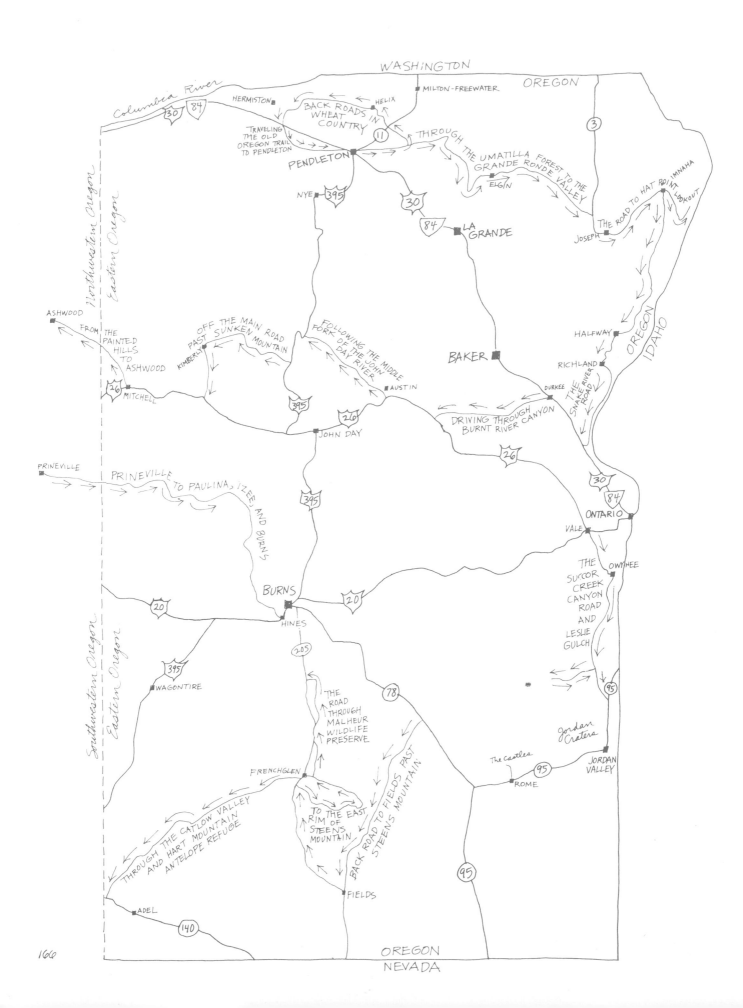

WASHINGTON

OREGON

Columbia River

30 84

HERMISTON

HELIX

MILTON-FREEWATER

3

BACK ROADS IN
WHEAT COUNTRY

TRAVELING
THE OLD
OREGON TRAIL
TO PENDLETON

11

THROUGH THE UMATILLA FOREST TO THE
GRANDE RONDE VALLEY

PENDLETON

NYE

395

30

IMNAHA

THE ROAD TO HAT POINT
LOOKOUT

ELGIN

84

LA GRANDE

JOSEPH

Northwestern Oregon

Eastern Oregon

ASHWOOD

FROM
THE
PAINTED
HILLS
TO
ASHWOOD

OFF THE MAIN ROAD
PAST SUNKEN
MOUNTAIN

FOLLOWING THE MIDDLE
FORK OF THE JOHN
DAY RIVER

HALFWAY

OREGON

IDAHO

26

MITCHELL

KIMBERLY

395

26

AUSTIN

BAKER

DURKEE

RICHLAND

THE SNAKE RIVER ROAD

JOHN DAY

DRIVING THROUGH
BURNT RIVER CANYON

26

30

PRINEVILLE

PRINEVILLE TO PAULINA, IZEE AND BURNS

395

84

ONTARIO

VALE

OWYHEE

THE
SUCCOR
CREEK
CANYON
ROAD
AND
LESLIE
GULCH

BURNS

20

20

HINES

205

Southwestern Oregon

Eastern Oregon

395

WAGONTIRE

78

THE
ROAD
THROUGH
MALHEUR
WILDLIFE
PRESERVE

95

Jordan
Craters

JORDAN
VALLEY

The Castles

95

ROME

FRENCHGLEN

TO THE EAST
RIM OF
STEENS
MOUNTAIN

BACK ROAD TO FIELDS PAST
STEENS MOUNTAIN

THROUGH THE CATLOW VALLEY
AND HART MOUNTAIN
ANTELOPE REFUGE

95

FIELDS

ADEL

140

OREGON

NEVADA

Eastern Oregon

The immensity of this region's mountains, canyons, rivers, plains and gorges, stretching out under a huge expanse of sky challenged my comprehension. Back roads here were longer, dustier, and often bumpier than those in western Oregon, but they were nevertheless just as well worth traveling. And it was like entering the "real" west with its cattle, coyotes, antelope, dust devils, cowboys, and tumbling-down early settlers' cabins.

Sunflower, Snake River road

Traveling the old Oregon Trail to Pendleton

Cara Neal said her barn had been painted with a
Bull Durham slogan in 1911, but within a year Dr. Pierce
came along with a better offer and the sign was
painted over.

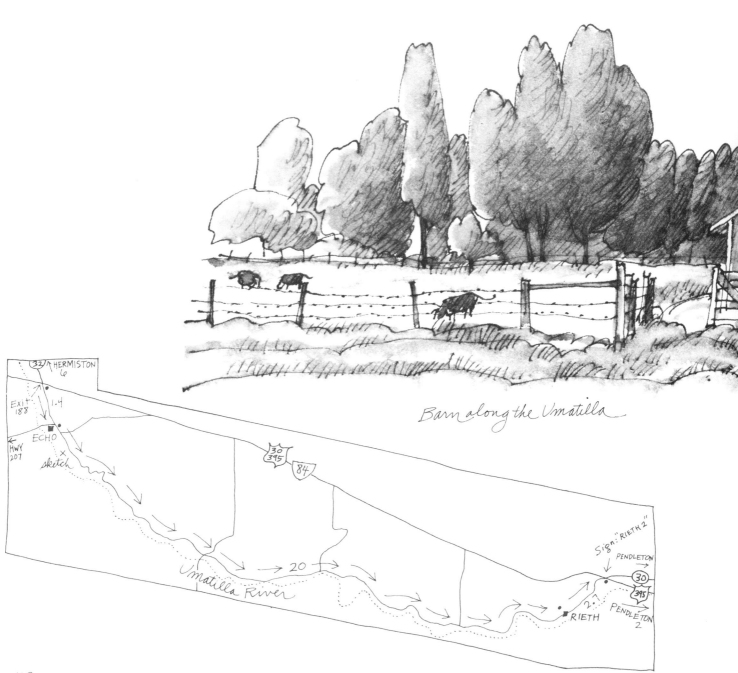

Barn along the Umatilla

The road past Echo was once the main
highway, but now only back road travelers can be
apprised of the doctor's Golden Medical Discovery.
The Umatilla runs past this road and
so do long, long freight trains.

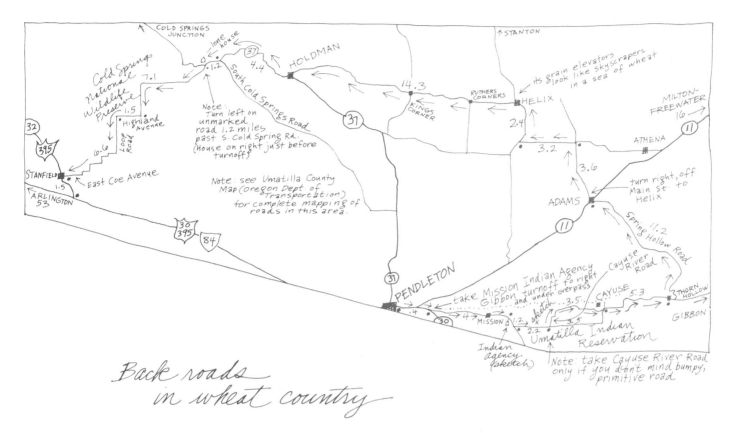

*Back roads
in wheat country*

On these roads long views of wheat
fields and the patterns that plowing them
makes delighted my eyes.
     A totem pole adorns the entrance
to the Bureau of Interior Umatilla
Indian Reservation. The Indian worker
I asked about its origin said that it
had been constructed in the early 1930s
by CCC camp laborers at nearby Squaw
Creek. The talents of many went
into its creation. It has been
repainted several times, noses have
been replaced, and the base repaired,
so that the CCC totem still stands
tall at reservation headquarters.

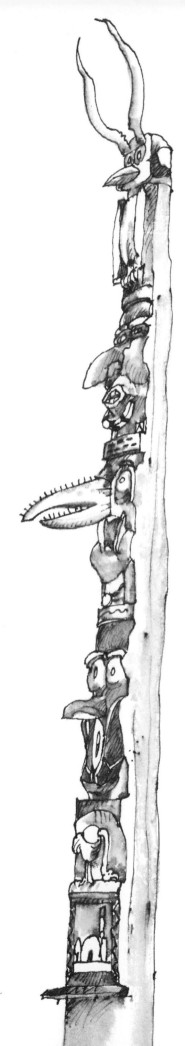

Totem at the
Umatilla Indian
agency

Wheat fields around Pendleton

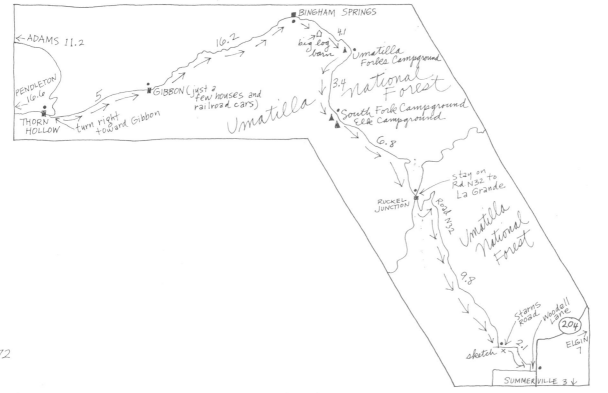

BINGHAM SPRINGS

← ADAMS 11.2

16.2

4.1

big log
barn

Umatilla
Forks Campground

PENDLETON
16.6

5

GIBBON (just a
few houses and
railroad cars)

*National
Forest*

3.4

Umatilla

THORN
HOLLOW

turn right
toward Gibbon

South Fork Campground
Elk Campground

6.8

Stay on
Rd N32 to
La Grande

RUCKEL
JUNCTION

Road N32

Umatilla
National
Forest

9.8

Starns
Road

Woodell
Lane

204

ELGIN
7

sketch ×

SUMMERVILLE 3 ↓

Through the Umatilla Forest to the Grande Ronde Valley

    By the time I reached Gibbon, forest trees were beginning to appear. I passed Bingham Springs, where there once had been a sulphur springs spa, and the Bar M Ranch with its great log barn.
    I continued on the mountain road through the forest to the spacious and fertile Grande Ronde Valley.

174

The Grande Ronde Valley

The road to
Hat Point Lookout

Stopping at the Ranger Station at Joseph to check on road conditions, I was handed a guide describing the trip to Hat Point. There was a popular store at Imnaha, where one could enjoy a cold drink before ascending to or descending from Hat Point. The road to the top was long and bumpy. The scenery, however, made it all worthwhile.

I climbed the 100 steps to the tiny cabin of Hat Point lookout tower where 7,072 feet above the earth's surface at sea level, I had a view of the Snake River in Hell's Canyon 1,250 feet below.

The view from Hat Point

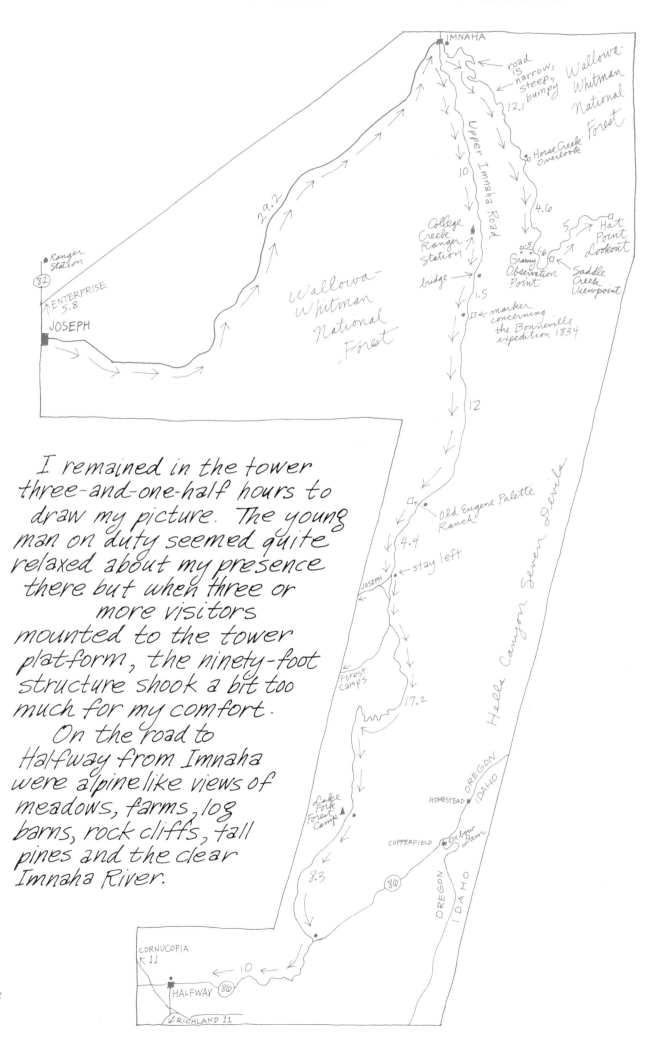

IMNAHA

road is narrow, steep, bumpy

Wallowa-Whitman National Forest

12.1

Horse Creek Overlook

Upper Imnaha Road

10

4.6

College Creek Ranger Station

5 → Hat Point Lookout

.5 1.6

Granny Observation Point

Saddle Creek Viewpoint

bridge →

1.5

← marker concerning the Bonneville expedition 1834

Wallowa-Whitman National Forest

Ranger Station

(82)

ENTERPRISE 5.8

JOSEPH

12

Old Eugene Palette Ranch

4.4

← stay left

JOSEPH

Hells Canyon Seven Devils

Forest Camps

17.2

I remained in the tower three-and-one-half hours to draw my picture. The young man on duty seemed quite relaxed about my presence there but when three or more visitors mounted to the tower platform, the ninety-foot structure shook a bit too much for my comfort.

On the road to Halfway from Imnaha were alpine-like views of meadows, farms, log barns, rock cliffs, tall pines and the clear Imnaha River.

Lake Fork Forest Camp

HOMESTEAD

OREGON IDAHO

COPPERFIELD Oxbow Dam

8.3

(86)

OREGON IDAHO

CORNUCOPIA ← 11

← 10 ←

HALFWAY (86)

↓ RICHLAND 11

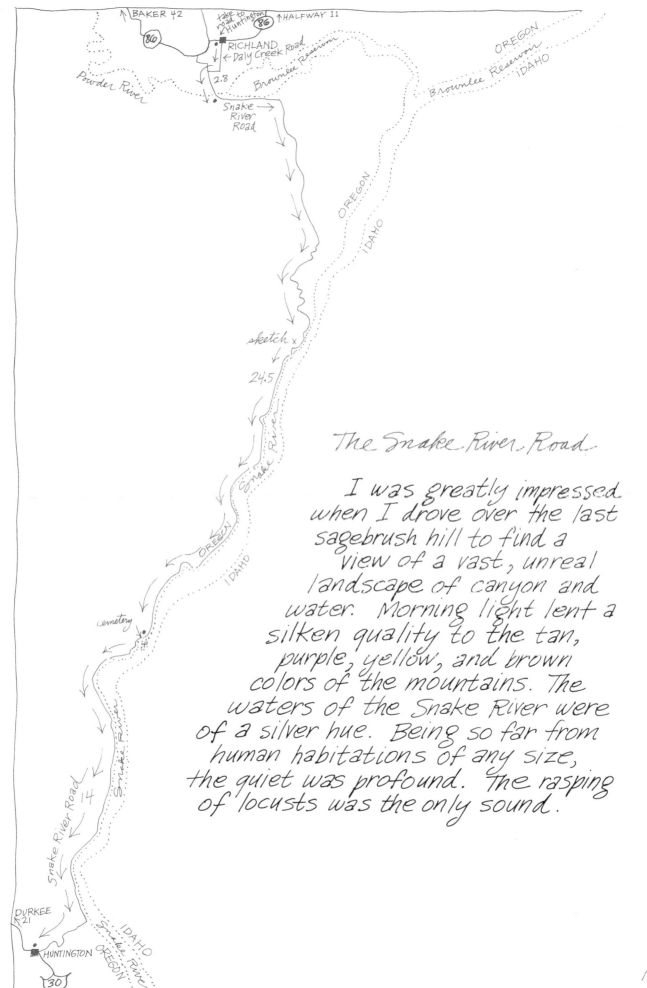

BAKER 42 ↑   take to road ↓Huntington ↑HALFWAY 11
86   86
RICHLAND
← Daly Creek Road
Powder River   2.8   Brownlee Reservoir   OREGON
Snake River Road →   Brownlee Reservoir   IDAHO
OREGON
IDAHO

sketch x
24.5

Snake River
OREGON
IDAHO

cemetery

Snake River Road 14   Snake River

DURKEE 21
HUNTINGTON   IDAHO   Snake River   OREGON
30
↓ONTARIO 30

The Snake River Road.

I was greatly impressed
when I drove over the last
sagebrush hill to find a
view of a vast, unreal
landscape of canyon and
water. Morning light lent a
silken quality to the tan,
purple, yellow, and brown
colors of the mountains. The
waters of the Snake River were
of a silver hue. Being so far from
human habitations of any size,
the quiet was profound. The rasping
of locusts was the only sound.

179

The Snake River Road along the Oregon-Idaho-border

Giant
blazing star

Driving through
Burnt River Canyon

I came upon many cattle
and sage grouse along the
road. The cattle would
stare, then turn and trot
ahead of me until I could
gently overtake them and
encourage them to one side.
A cowboy rounding up a small
herd told me "Ah'm jes'
taken' 'em up the road."
    I sketched a flower along
here, the giant blazing star,
which has five white starlike
petals that open at night.

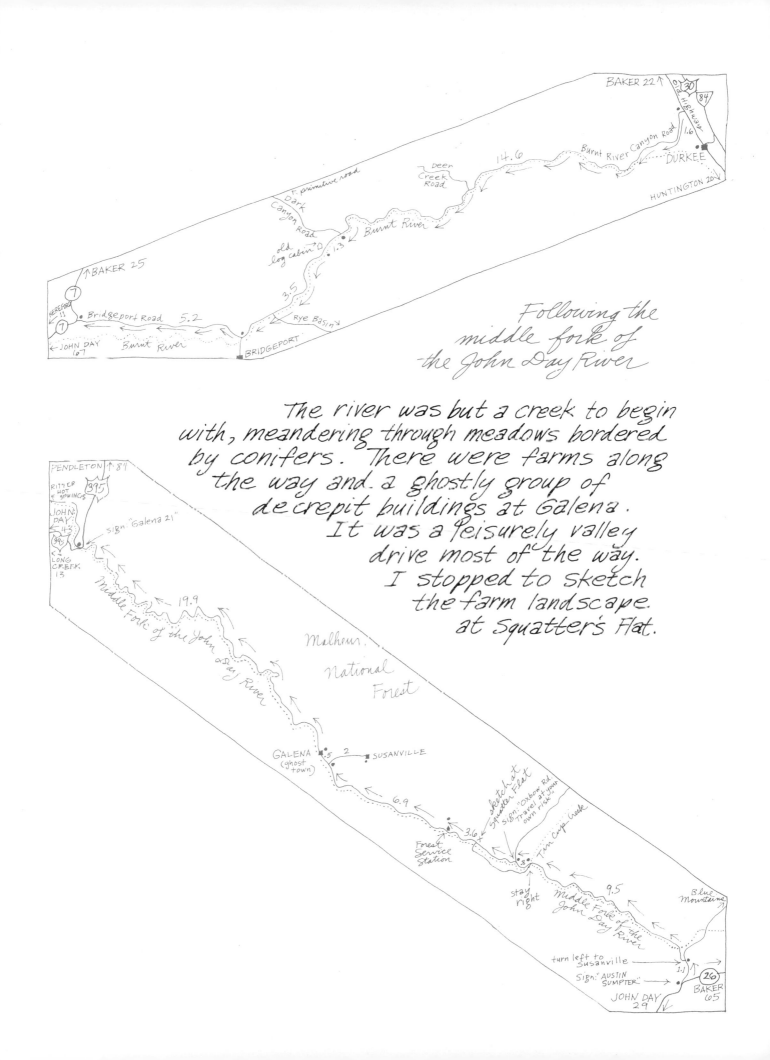

BAKER 22 ↑

Old Highway 30

84

Burnt River Canyon Road 1.6

DURKEE

HUNTINGTON 20↓

14.6

Deer Creek Road

↑ primitive road

Dark Canyon Road

old log cabin □ • 1.3 Burnt River

3.5

↑ BAKER 25

7

HEREFORD 11

7

Bridgeport Road 5.2

Rye Basin ↘

← JOHN DAY 67

Burnt River

BRIDGEPORT

Following the middle fork of the John Day River

The river was but a creek to begin with, meandering through meadows bordered by conifers. There were farms along the way and a ghostly group of decrepit buildings at Galena. It was a leisurely valley drive most of the way. I stopped to sketch the farm landscape at Squatter's Flat.

PENDLETON ↑ 84

RITTER HOT SPRINGS

395

JOHN DAY 43

399

← LONG CREEK 13

sign "Galena 21"

Middle Fork of the John Day River

19.9

Malheur National Forest

GALENA (ghost town) • .5 2 ● SUSANVILLE

6.9

Forest Service Station

3.6

sketch at Squatter Flat

sign: "Oxbow Rd. Travel at your own risk."

.8

Tin Cup Creek

stay right

Middle Fork of the John Day River

9.5

Blue Mountains

turn left to Susanville

sign: "AUSTIN SUMPTER"

1.1

26

BAKER 65

JOHN DAY 29 ↓

Farm at Squatter's Flat along the middle fork of the John Day River

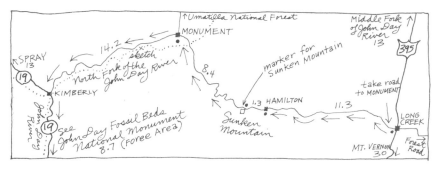

Off the main road past Sunken Mountain

In Oregon some back roads are much like highways. This fast back road passed a view of Sunken Mountain, which, did indeed seem to slip in the middle. The slow-paced village of Monument is surrounded by impressive rock formations. Just beyond the town I sketched the north fork of the John Day River as it flowed through the mountains.

North fork of the John Day River, near Monument

From the Painted Hills to Ashwood

I drew the ochres, yellows and reds of Painted Hills in the early morning. It was a challenge to represent so much color in black and white!

MADRAS 33
MADRAS 35
ASHWOOD
↓ Stud Horse Creek
6.9
↑ANTELOPE 17
Sign: "Mitchell 40 Horse Heaven Burnt Ranch"
10.8
6.5
HORSE HEAVEN
Cherry Creek Ranch
ford Cherry Creek
2
dramatic scenery
6.3
Byrds Point
John Day River
log bridge
5.9
Sign: ASHWOOD 36"
sketch
Painted Hills State Park
↓ 1.3
sketch
5.6
6.1
FOSSIL 46 ↑
26
26
207
PRINEVILLE 44
4.1
MITCHELL

The scenery only got better as I traveled the road to Ashwood. Views of Bridge Creek Valley, Byrd's Point, and the John Day River were a pleasure to behold. The road became more primitive after the last farm, until it reached Horse Heaven. It would not be good to travel this portion in wet weather.

Painted Hills

Prineville to Paulina,
Izee and Burns

Before I began to explore the
back roads of Crook County,
I sketched the architecture
of the county court house.
Built of native stone and brick in
1909, it is now a
historical monument.
There was the Crooked River,
farmland, and the mountains
of Ochoco National Forest
to see on this trip.
Paulina had a
frontier town look
with its little church and
assortment of houses
clustered near the
General Store.

Crook County Courthouse, Prineville

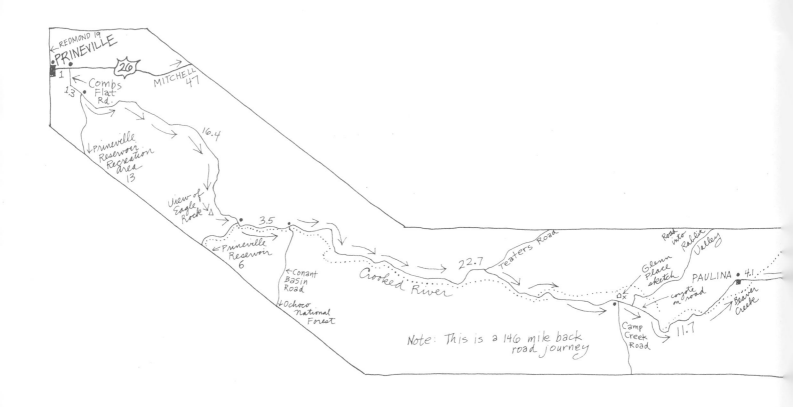

The Succor Creek Canyon Road and Leslie Gulch

The scenery was rugged with purplish brown crags that surrounded us campers in Succor Creek Canyon. It was late in the day. I cooked some dinner at the campground and watched the moon go down behind the high canyon walls. The only sound was cooing of doves from their perches among the high rocks.

Early next morning on the way to Leslie Gulch a herd of deer, including four large bucks, bounded gracefully across the road.

Leslie Gulch was a magnificent natural cathedral offering a treasury of highly colored and lofty rock creations for me to enjoy.

There were also the Jordan Craters close to the town of Jordan Valley and, near Rome, "the castles" to see.

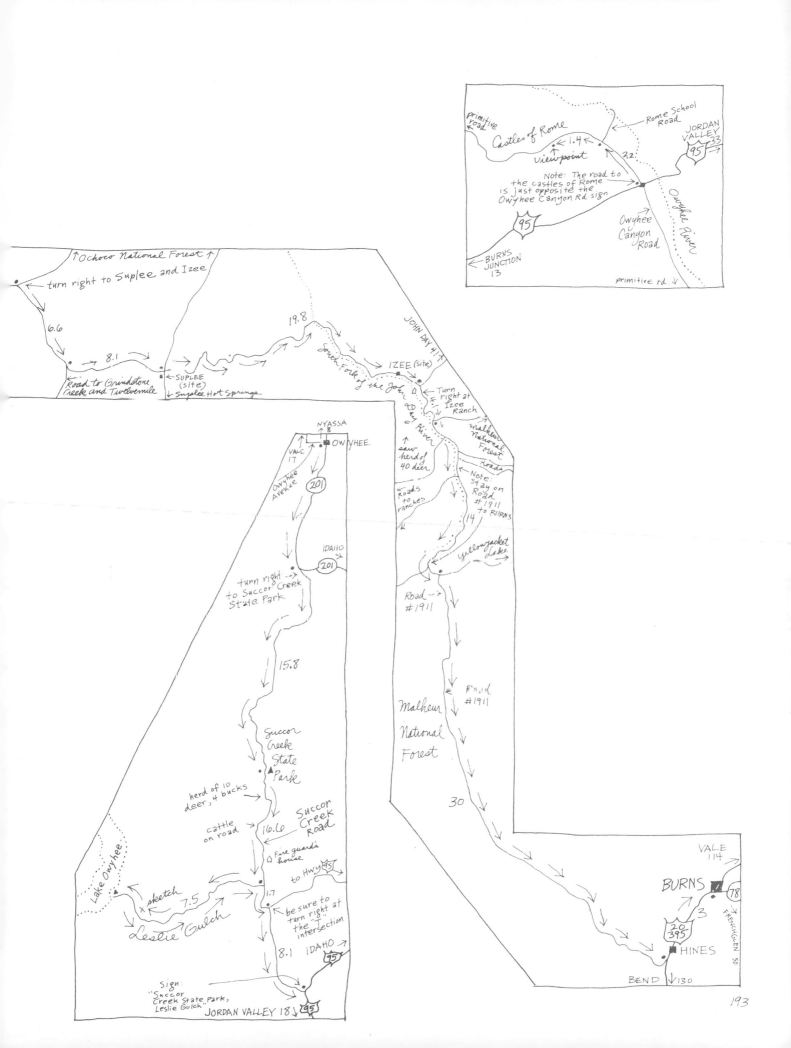

↑Ochoco National Forest↑
←turn right to Suplee and Izee

6.6

8.1

19.8

South Fork of the John

IZEE (site)

JOHN DAY HI WY

←Road to Grindstone
Creek and Twelvemile

←SUPLEE (site)
↓Suplee Hot Springs

Turn right at Izee Ranch

Malheur National Forest

↑ saw herd of 40 deer

Day River

Roads

Note: Stay on Road #1911 to BURNS

14

Roads to ranches

Yellowjacket lake

Castles of Rome

Rome School Road

JORDAN VALLEY
95 / 33

primitive road

1.4
viewpoint

22

Note: The road to the castles of Rome is just opposite the Owyhee Canyon Rd sign

Owyhee River

95

Owyhee Canyon Road

BURNS JUNCTION 13

primitive rd. ↓

NYASSA 8

VALE 17

OWYHEE

Owyhee Avenue

201

IDAHO 201

turn right → to Succor Creek State Park

15.8

Succor Creek State Park

herd of 10 deer, 4 bucks

cattle on road

16.6

Succor Creek Road

Road #1911

Primd #1911

Malheur National Forest

30

Lake Owyhee

sketch

7.5

Leslie Gulch

1.7

Fire guard's house

to Hwy 95

be sure to turn right at the "T" intersection

8.1 IDAHO 95

Sign: "Succor Creek State Park, Leslie Gulch"
JORDAN VALLEY 18 ↓ 95

VALE 114

BURNS 78

3

20 395

HINES

FRENCHGLEN 50

BEND ↓130

Leslie Gulch

Back road to Fields
past Steens Mountain

The great mass of Steens
   Mountain rose to incredible
heights from the valley floor
   along this road. There were
occasional farms, and the
large Alvord Ranch. I found
it comforting to know that
I wasn't entirely alone on
   this sixty-five-mile stretch
   of dirt road!
      Farther on there was a big, big view of the
Alvord Desert and the mighty 9,000-foot Steens
Mountain towering above.

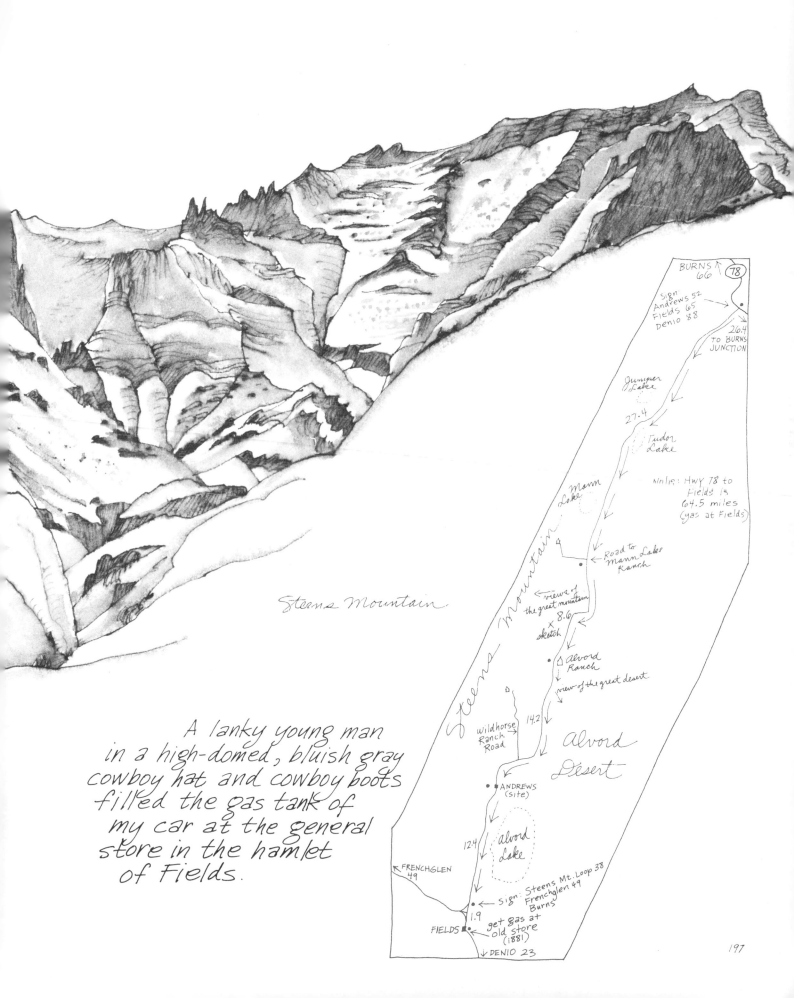

Steens Mountain

A lanky young man
in a high-domed, bluish gray
cowboy hat and cowboy boots
filled the gas tank of
my car at the general
store in the hamlet
of Fields.

BURNS↑ 78
66

Sign:
Andrews 52
Fields 65
Denio 88

26.4
TO BURNS
JUNCTION

Juniper
Lake

27.4

Tudor
Lake

Miles: Hwy 78 to
Fields 18
64.5 miles
(gas at Fields)

Mann
Lake

Road to Mann Lake
Ranch

Steens Mountain

views of
the great mountain

8.6

× sketch

Alvord
Ranch

view of the great desert

14.2

Alvord
Desert

Wildhorse
Ranch
Road

ANDREWS
(site)

12.4

Alvord
Lake

FRENCHGLEN
49

Sign: Steens Mt. Loop 38
Frenchglen 49
Burns

1.9

get gas at
old store
(1881)

FIELDS

↓DENIO 23

197

To the east rim of Steens Mountain

At the base of the Steens Mountain Loop was the tiny community of Frenchglen and its comfortable hotel. Still in operation, it was built in 1916 by the famous local cattle baron of that time, Pete French.

The drive up Steens Mountain was deceptive in that it was such a gradual slope I didn't realize I was achieving great altitude. Passing from sagebrush country to juniper, to groves of aspen and to alpine wildflower strewn meadow told me I was certainly gaining altitude. Higher up there were spectacular views of glaciated valleys and from the east rim the large vista of the Alvord Desert over a mile below and all the land beyond.

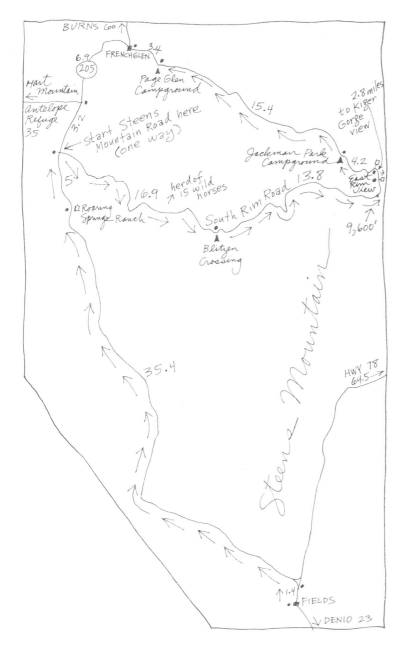

Map labels:
- BURNS 60
- FRENCHGLEN 3.4
- 205
- 6.9
- Hart Mountain
- Antelope Refuge 35
- 3"N
- Page Glen Campground
- Start Steens Mountain Road here (one way)
- 15.4
- 2.8 miles to Kiger Gorge view
- Jackman Park Campground 4.2
- East Rim View
- herd of 15 wild horses
- 16.9
- South Rim Road 13.8
- 9,600'
- 5
- Roaring Springs Ranch
- Blitzen Crossing
- Steens Mountain
- 35.4
- HWY 78 64.5
- 1.4 FIELDS
- DENIO 23

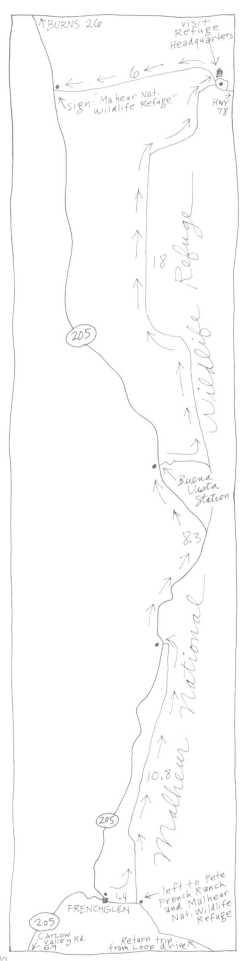

The road through
Malheur Wildlife Refuge

Though it was not March or
April, when the largest
concentrations of birds
are present, I was able to
see many varieties. These
included Great Blue Herons,
White Pelicans, Trumpeter
Swans, Canada Geese,
Long-billed Curlews, Great
Egrets, Snowy Egrets, and
many kinds of ducks
and hawks.

President Theodore
Roosevelt established this
preserve in 1908. Ponds
and crops are managed for
the benefit of wildlife.

It was good to see a
place dedicated to man's
concern for nature. What
would our earth be like
without birds of all variety?

Trumpeter Swan

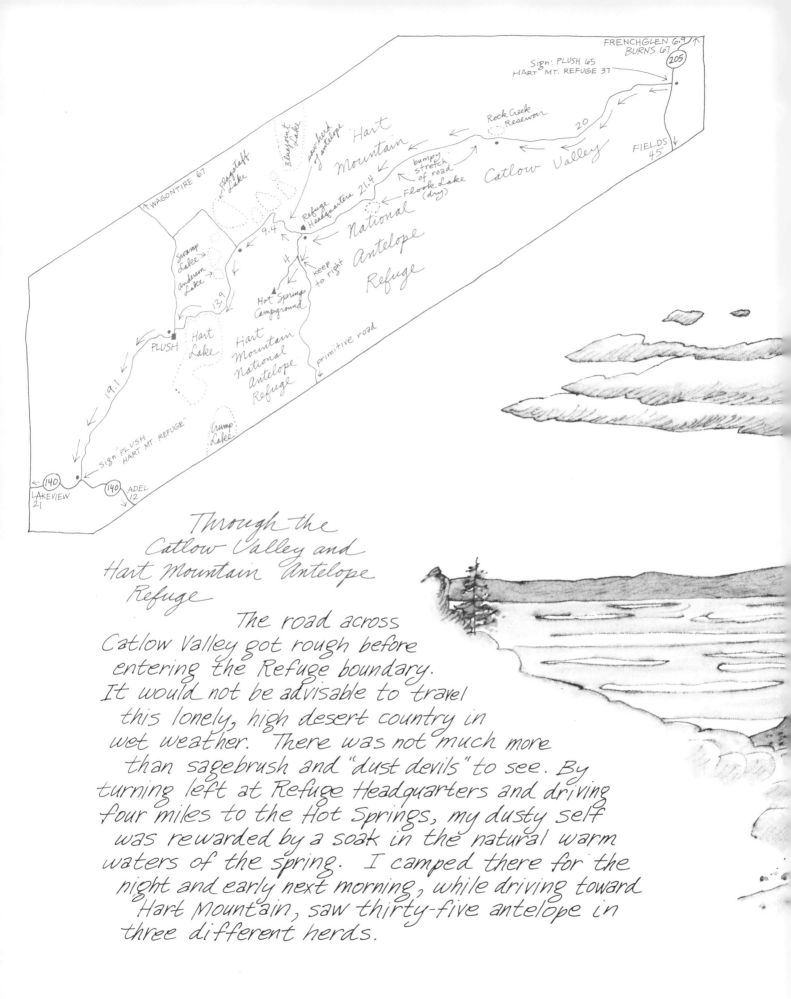

Through the Catlow Valley and Hart Mountain Antelope Refuge

The road across Catlow Valley got rough before entering the Refuge boundary. It would not be advisable to travel this lonely, high desert country in wet weather. There was not much more than sagebrush and "dust devils" to see. By turning left at Refuge Headquarters and driving four miles to the Hot Springs, my dusty self was rewarded by a soak in the natural warm waters of the spring. I camped there for the night and early next morning, while driving toward Hart Mountain, saw thirty-five antelope in three different herds.

Frightened by my
vehicle they would
run, then abruptly
change direction,
as if to confuse a
hunter's aim. It was
a thrill to see such
beautiful animals
in the wild.

View from Hart Mountain

Otis, my back
road advisor

Thoughts while traveling

It adds much to the remembrance of a place
to talk to local people. They would often
introduce themselves to me while I was sketching,
an opportunity to talk that I always welcomed.
I would also stop in the General Store to
shop and perhaps quench my thirst by drinking
something on the spot, returning the empty bottle to
the counter. Sometimes just being in a place for awhile
generates conversation. Checking road directions or
getting advice on what to see locally is another usually
successful way to begin a conversation with a stranger.

I believe that if one loves the earth and respects mankind one does not defile the land by throwing litter from an automobile.

I stayed in many motels in my travels through Oregon and those I appreciated most were neat, clean smelling and located away from highway noise.. The owner's friendliness, flowers in the room (even just one or two) and a picture on the wall of good quality would make my home away from home all I could ask for.

Coming off a slow back road trip onto a busy highway, it is sometimes shocking to realize how fast and recklessly we have suddenly begun to travel.

I've become aware that the faster I drive the more I become an asphalt watcher. Driving is especially interesting and fun at slow speeds, for then I can enjoy the scenery. If there are many curves in the road I simply slow down even more. And on back roads I've noticed that many other drivers also seem to relax and enjoy the drive and the sights.

I'm remembering the route to Olallie Lake, a bumpy and twisted single lane road. The scenery was so close I could almost touch it. Ten miles per hour was maximum speed and though it was a narrow road, I knew that any traffic coming toward me was also limited by that speed so there was little likelihood of an accident.

I hope that road never changes. As soon as pavement and a double lane are put in, the road will be straightened, speed increased, and we will once again become asphalt watchers.

On dirt and gravel back roads I slowed down when meeting another vehicle to minimize the dust. I hoped that other drivers would do the same. Most often they did and we would both wave a greeting as we passed.

I wish more of Oregon's scenic back roads were in the one-way direction. Then they would not have to be wide, and more contact with nature would be felt. I'm thinking of the Grayback Ridge Motor Nature Trail near Crater Lake, a one-way road where I enjoyed a relaxing drive. I had more time to take in the sights than I would have otherwise. As Oregon's back roads are broadened and straightened for the needs of commerce, nature seems to retreat on all sides.

I found that many other drivers on back roads will wave as they go by. This is particularly true on less traveled roads. It is a wonderful way to indicate friendliness when an exchange of words isn't possible.

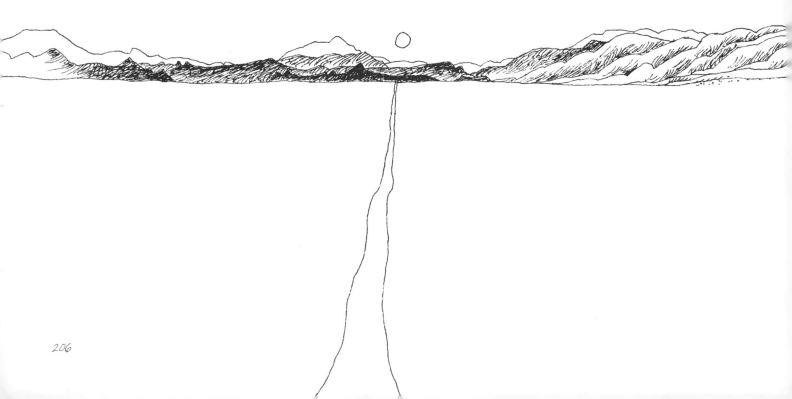

While I was sketching the Painted Hills, a young man stopped his car, snapped a picture with his camera, and drove away. It made me feel fortunate for my way of recording what I see. When he arrived, I had been drawing and observing for only a half-hour and my mind and body had already received much from the experience. There is a rapport with nature that occurs when I stop at a beautiful location long enough to draw. A feeling of peace enfolds me, and I seem to be truly interacting with the earth. (That is, at least until I drop ink on the paper, the temperature becomes intolerable, or ants crawl up my legs and bite.)

As functional and practical as they are, mobile homes are sometimes jarring to my sense of aesthetics. This is especially so when I see one prominently fixed in some lovely Oregon meadow or next to an elegant barn. I immediately feel like stopping to plant shrubs, trees, and flowers, to somewhat shroud its all too "box-car-looking" proportions.

Some owners of property along the back roads have posted large, forbidding "No Trespassing" signs. The reason for this is mostly an intense fear of grass or forest fires that could be started innocently enough by hikers or hunters who smoke, or campers who leave untended fires. We should all respect the demands of private property where they appear.

Index